CATCH BA

THE ANGLING TIMES LIBRARY

CATCH BARBEL

WITH

JOHN WILSON

B☘XTREE

in association with
ANGLING TIMES

First published in the UK 1992
by Boxtree Limited, 36 Tavistock Street,
London WC2E 7PB

1 3 5 7 9 10 8 6 4 2

© (text and photographs) John Wilson 1992
© (illustrations) Boxtree Limited 1992

Illustrations by David Batten
Cover design by Dave Goodman/Millions Design
Design by Peter Ward
Editor Helen Douglas-Cooper

Set in 10/13pt Linotron Bembo
Typeset by Cambrian Typesetters, Frimley
Colour origination by Fotographics, Hong Kong
Printed and bound in the UK by Richard Clay, Bungay

A catalogue record for this book is available
from the British Library.

ISBN 1 85283 153 7

AUTHOR'S ACKNOWLEDGEMENTS

No angling writer can produce a book without consider-
able help from others. Allow me therefore to thank the
editing and design team, the mates who leave their own
fishing to photograph me, and a very special thank you to
good friend Dave Batten who has made such a fine job of
the line drawings.

CONTENTS

INTRODUCTION

IF there is a down side to barbel fishing, it is that our river systems do not contain enough of this fine battler. Fortunately the species is presently growing to a good average size and proliferating along every river into which it has been introduced during the past few decades.

Much of the credit for this goes to *Angling Times* who, in co-operation with the Severn River Board, organized the stocking of the first-ever barbel into the mighty River Severn back in 1956. *Angling Times* also helped stock barbel into the Trent where, years earlier, they had flourished but had more recently become seriously depleted through pollution. Barbel were also put into the Bristol Avon which, like the Severn, is now a fabulous barbel fishery and improving all the time. In all probability, the Severn now holds the largest concentration of barbel in the British Isles. Other rivers stocked with the help of *Angling Times* are the Nene and the upper reaches of the Welland.

The result of the barbel's widespread success is that, after carp and pike, it provides the freshwater enthusiast with his largest potential catch. It is a fish that necessitates no small measure of skill to extract from the fast, swirling waters of clear-flowing rivers. And it is a fish that, pound for pound, is one of the hardest-fighting freshwater river fish in the world. No wonder everyone wants to catch barbel.

CHAPTER ONE

THE
SPECIES

BARBEL
(Barbus barbus)

With its unique physical shape producing exhilarating speed and strength, the barbel is the most exciting adversary in British freshwater fishing in the opinion of many fishermen.

It is a member of the cyprinidae, or carp family of freshwater fish, by far the largest single group in Europe. Indeed, it is no coincidence that its powerful, elongated shape – round in cross-section except for its flat stomach – resembles that of a long drawn-out carp. It also shares many of the carp's physical characteristics and habits. As well as having four sensory barbels or barbules – one pair at the very point of the snout, the other situated way back at the rear of the top lip – and a protrusible, hoover-like mouth, the barbel also possesses a strong serrated spine at the start of its dorsal fin, exactly like the carp. Care must be taken when netting and retaining barbel, for this spine all too easily becomes entangled, and can be broken in all types of netting larger than micromesh (see Retaining Barbel, p. 61).

Like the grayling, the barbel is a lover of well-oxygenated river water, and if it has the choice, it prefers to occupy the fastest runs over a gravel or clean sandy bottom. However, it also thrives in slow-moving river systems, and, also like the grayling, it can even exist in clear, pure stillwaters with a high level of dissolved oxygen. For instance, I know of several gravel pits and reservoir complexes along the River Lea valley that, contrary to popular belief, contain good numbers of barbel. These fish even manage to reproduce successfully

Sleek and powerful with large fins, the barbel is exceptionally well-equipped for holding station in the strongest currents. Its vacuum-type mouth and four long sensory barbules enable it to root among the gravel in search of shrimps, molluscs and tiny fish.

each spring by using the fast-water run-off and intake weirs connecting one complex to another. Generally speaking, however, the barbel is a river fish.

In overall colouration few fish, except perhaps the grayling, blend in against the bottom so efficiently as the barbel. Even when looking through polaroid glasses into crystal-clear fast water where the river-bed consists of clean gravel, it is often possible to see barbel hugging the bottom only by training your eyes to search for the subtle orange hue of their pectoral and pelvic fins. In fact, had Mother Nature not given the barbel such large and distinctly shaped pectorals and a flat belly, which together provide it with enormous suction power for anchoring itself to the bottom in fast currents, it would be almost impossible to locate them visually.

The barbel's front end when viewed from above is triangular and skate-like, and it has similar powers of adhesion as the skate. Such is the power of even small barbel during the initial stages of a fight, that the line feels as if it is being 'ironed' to the river-bed.

When chub and barbel of more or less similar size are mixed together in runs between beds of streamer weed and their front ends are not immediately visible, the barbel are easily distinguished by their large, forked tails. The top lobe is sharply pointed while the lower is rounded.

Out of the water, the barbel's body seems quite warm in colour. The back can vary from an even olive-brown to

Even modest-sized barbel have immense strength and provide exciting sport throughout the season, especially during the warmer months, when they feed aggressively.

brown-grey, which blends into flanks of pale brass and a matt white belly. Its scales are small, firmly embedded, and lie very flat to the body, with only the finest covering of protective mucus. However, even small barbel are difficult to hold, being wiry and extremely powerful. An adult, specimen barbel in the 9–12 lb range measures somewhere between 28 and 36 in, and in terms of its length to weight ratio it is one of the lightest freshwater species after the eel. Only the pike shares a similar weight to length ratio.

In many rivers barbel tend to shoal according to size.

Most are in the 3–6 lb class, and anything exceeding 8 lb is a fine specimen. This is not to say, however, that a lone huge barbel will not be seen among a group of 2–3 pounders. They are a very gregarious species, and fight to the last with unbelievable power, whatever their size.

Only during the barbel's young stage, when it is just a few inches long, is it liable to be confused with loach and gudgeon, both of which look very similar and could at first glance be taken for immature barbel. If you look carefully, however, you will notice that the gudgeon has been provided with only two barbels protruding from its upper lip, compared to the barbel's four, while the loach has no less than six.

CHAPTER TWO

ABOUT BARBEL

FEEDING

By nature barbel feed with greater confidence from dusk onwards and during the hours of darkness. Barbel fishermen soon become aware of this when fish that have been seen to refuse the hook bait during daylight suddenly produce slamming bites as the sun starts to go down and light values rapidly decrease.

This is not to say that they will not feed avidly even during bright sunshine, because they do, especially when sheltered beneath sanctuary or habitat swims where they can constantly nip in and out – gravel runs beneath overhead canopies of cut weed or flotsam, narrow sandy runs between scattered beds of tall bullrushes, or clear runs beneath low, overhanging willow or alder branches, where the sun's rays cannot directly reach to stimulate weed growth in otherwise heavily weeded parts of the river. Through regular introductions of loose feed such as hempseed, tares, maggots, corn and the like, barbel in these ideal swims can be tempted into feeding all day long during the summer, and especially the autumn.

Once winter frosts start to reduce weed cover, barbel become far less spread out. As they shoal in much tighter groups, pinpoint accuracy in assessing their position, and in your casting, becomes all important and can make the difference between bites and no bites (see Location, page 25).

Various conditions can trigger the barbel into feeding aggressively: a rising river, times when clear water starts to colour up; when the flow suddenly starts increasing due to a weir or hatch opening upstream; and during periods of consistently high air temperatures in what is generally

As the late afternoon sun starts to go down, barbel enthusiasts on this wide, popular reach of the prolific River Severn at Atcham wait expectantly, knowing full well that their quarry will leave the massive beds of flowing weed to feed in earnest on the gravel shallows.

considered to be the coldest part of the winter. Any prolonged mild spell brought about by warm winds calls out for barbel fishing.

The last few weeks of the season is invariably the best time for seeking winter barbel and finding them in a feeding mood. Though they will bite even in extremely cold water, once pinpointed, winter barbel fishing can prove to be a slow pastime, especially in rivers where they are not prolific, and at that time are certainly no match for the inexperienced.

In some respects feeding is down to competition. In large rivers, such as the mighty River Severn, where shoals of barbel number dozens, even hundreds of fish, there is always a fish or two willing to break the rules and have a go due to the tough level of competition for food within the shoal. They will do this almost regardless of river and weather conditions. On the other hand, a group of seven plump barbel inhabiting a choice lie in the rich upper reaches of the River Kennet, where there is no shortage of natural food, may not be inclined to feed on your hook bait until light, water and weather conditions are completely favourable.

This powerful, rather enigmatic fish is exceptionally

well equipped for grubbing about along the river-bed, where the majority of its food exists. Although barbel do occasionally take food close to the surface among dense beds of rooted weeds such as the water crowfoot (the distinct carp-like sucking noises they make can sometimes be heard at night), they are bottom-feeders *par excellence*.

Situated immediately above its thick, fleshy· lips (so tough that few hooks ever pull out) the barbel's long whiskers, conveniently equipped with super-sensitive taste pads at the tips, probe between the particles of sand and gravel in search of its daily diet, which consists of shrimps, snails, crayfish and aquatic insect larvae. Barbel also eat small fish like minnows, loach, bullheads, gudgeon, lampreys and even their own kind, all of which are snuffed up and quickly minced by the powerful pharyngeal (throat) teeth into pulp for swallowing. A small, freshly killed fish makes a fine offering for barbel (see Baits, page 73), especially during the early season when they have easy access to fry shoals in the warm shallows.

Barbel are renowned for leaving the sanctuary of weed beds or deep daytime retreats beneath undercuts and tree roots under the cloak of darkness in order to forage along the bottom of ridiculously shallow water for crustaceans

With its orange pectoral and pelvic fins active, the unmistakeable shape of a barbel can be identified as it competes with a shoal of chub for the fisherman's loose feed on the sandy bottom beneath a trail of streamer weed.

and small fish – areas so shallow you would not believe they are frequented by barbel at night.

An example of this, in a particular swim on the Old River Lea at Enfield Lock, springs to mind. During my teens I regularly fished there for barbel after dark from June through until October. The long, wide gravel run of no more than 1 ft deep, situated immediately upstream of a deep hole beneath an old railway bridge, was completely empty during the hours of daylight. Each and every pebble (along with the inevitable beer bottle) could be seen on the bottom, and the only fish in sight were shoals of minnows and immature gudgeon. The barbel were obviously very well aware of this, because whether I pre-baited for a few evenings with cubes of meat and cheese paste or not, once darkness set in quite suddenly the rod would arch over, accompanied by an enormous swirl on the surface. Once my eyes had become adjusted to the dark, I could sometimes even make out the furrows of several other fish as they vacated the swim and shot off downstream in panic leaving the hooked barbel to battle it out alone. I know that the spot where I hooked those barbel (never more than two in an evening) was no more than 1 ft deep because once temperatures dropped as winter advanced and the barbel were no longer willing to vacate their daytime swims, I used to wade out to stand in exactly the same spot in order to present float tackle to chub lying beneath an overhanging willow on the opposite bank. Strangely, I never once hooked into a chub at night while fishing the gravel shallows for barbel, despite there being less than 10 yd between the two areas.

When barbel are feeding really aggressively, they can be seen with their noses tilted downwards, rooting along the bottom, overturning stones and regularly twisting over, conveniently showing a long brassy flash of their flank – a most heartening visual pointer for those searching the fast, deep runs through polaroid glasses.

Born with a long conical nose, the barbel loses sight of its food long before it hoovers it up, and so characteristically moves it head from side to side in an agitated manner in order to centre the food immediately prior to swallowing. This explains why those who hold the line between thumb and forefinger and 'touch ledger' when barbel fishing can feel a sandpapery sensation on the line a moment or two before the rod arches over in that typical slamming bite for which barbel are famous. The barbel's long whiskers hit against the line as the barbel centres the bait before sucking it in.

This I have witnessed on numerous occasions when scuba-diving along the bottom in the clear water of my local rivers Wensum and Yare, among shoals of barbel that show not the slightest sign of fear provided that I approach slowly. In fact, it is not unusual to lie there almost as one of the shoal. The barbel even permit the diver to twiddle their whiskers and gently caress them. They really are quite unlike any other species I have ever encountered while diving in either fresh or salt water, anywhere in the world.

Many species can be tamed by regularly feeding them underwater, but barbel are different. They are naturally friendly and approachable when visited in their own world. I can remember several years ago now one particular September's evening, when enjoying a dive along the upper Wensum with my old buddy, Sid Johnson, that illustrates this perfectly. We were diving in one of the most prolific big-barbel lengths of the Wensum at Drayton, where only a few weeks before, friend Nobby Clarke had taken from below a huge overhanging willow a superb barbel of exactly 12¼ lb on link-ledgered sweetcorn.

By sheer coincidence Nobby was out walking the stretch along the bank while Sid and I were slowly making our way downstream, studying the bottom contours and looking for barbel and chub. Nobby happened to ask if we could keep an eye out for the big barbel he had caught, easily recognizable by a distinct, lumpy anal fin, a ridge along the upper lobe of its tail and a black spot close to its right eye.

Incidentally, most of the large barbel in the upper Wensum are known fish. Through various characteristic markings, each specimen is considered an individual to the many specialist anglers who pursue them regularly, just as carp and pike are instantly recognized in many of the more popular fisheries.

Continuing on downstream just 50 yd from where we left Nobby crouching high in the boughs of the willow, shielding his polaroids from the evening sun, we came

Barbel are attracted to the fast, bubbly water of weir-pools. John caught this one on ledgered cheese paste from the Royalty Fishery in Christchurch, Hampshire. Note the long, conical snout, which is put to good use in locating both its natural food and the angler's bait.

upon the very barbel he had recently caught. Looking at least one quarter larger than actual size, as all fish appear to the human eye when viewed underwater through the glass of a face-mask, that barbel looked absolutely enormous. It lay perfectly motionless on the bottom in 8 ft of water in a really slow-moving swim, its head buried in a clump of ribbon weed. It allowed me to support its body gently while we slowly rose to the surface. My plan was to show Nobby that his prize catch was alive and well, but the barbel had other ideas and leapt from my grasp halfway up. I had no way of knowing then that I too would catch that very same barbel several years later, a further ½ mile downstream on a misty November night after pre-baiting a shallow run on a bend for several days with stewed hempseed. Time had not increased the fish's weight during the intervening years, as one might have expected, for it tipped the scales at 1 oz under 12 lb, but it was Nobby's barbel all right.

Barbel tend to fluctuate, or free wheel, in weight at various times of the year, exactly like carp, and even from one year to the next – facts that have emerged from my

studies of the Wensum's stock of double-figure barbel for over 15 years. Several of these large fish, again just like carp from popular fisheries, are caught with surprising regularity. This tends to give the impression that the whole of the upper Wensum is one long barbel river, but this is simply not the case. The same, easily recognizable old barbel are being caught time and time again.

One such barbel, a female that weighed 10 lb 14 oz when I first caught her and 12¾ lb several years later, to the best of my knowledge provided at least twenty anglers with their first double-figure barbel. This particular, exceptionally obliging barbel has given me some idea as to how long the species might live, because I first weighed it in at over 10 lb for a friend some 13 years ago. No doubt it was one of the young fish introduced from the River Severn in the early 1970s, which puts it at a minimum of 20 years of age. Who knows – barbel share so many of the carp's characteristics, perhaps they too enjoy longevity. And as carp regularly live to between 30 and 50 years, I cannot see a lifespan of 30 years being out of the question for the barbel.

Old friends meet. Despite the pounding rain, John smiles, having instantly recognized a particular, large barbel that he has previously caught from the River Wensum. 'Known', recognizable barbel can, when caught repeatedly, give a false impression of the river's stock to those who don't know the river.

REPRODUCTION

To observe numbers of barbel gathered on the vast, gravelly shallows during the late spring in readiness for the reproduction cycle is one of the most pleasurable highlights of the closed season. Most fish work their way upriver from their respective habitats to the weedy, gravel shallows and bubbly water, where spawning takes place en masse. And in a prolific barbel river, there could be hundreds of fish crammed together into the tiniest area during this time.

The shallows immediately downstream of mill and weir-pools are usually prime spawning areas because of the well-oxygenated water running speedily over the gravel beds. And these are the first spots to visit if you wish to witness the barbel's spawning ritual. Confluences are well used for spawning, too.

This annual event usually happens during the latter part of April or early May, with the males becoming distinct from the females through the white tubercles that appear over their heads and back. It is in fact the only time of the year when there appears to be any physical difference between the sexes. The female – whose belly is now heavily swollen with eggs, is attended by groups of smaller male fish that quickly gather around when she is ready to spawn, bumping into her flanks with their rough (tubercle-covered) noses and shoulders to stimulate her to release the eggs. Even large females are sometimes heaved with such force by the eager males that the upper part of their bodies can be seen above the surface. Fertilization is almost instant. Milt from the energetic males is distributed in a cloud over the small yellow eggs as they tumble downstream, sticking to the stones and rooted weeds. Incubation takes up to 14 days depending upon the water temperature, following which the young barbel emerge into an extremely hostile world.

During their early life, most fall prey to other fish, chub in particular, while the barbel itself is renowned, like all cypinids, for consuming much of its own spawn and fry. This is a natural and very efficient inbuilt safety mechanism and insurance policy that prevents over-population of a water by the species.

DISTRIBUTION

Barbel are not extensively distributed throughout the British Isles. They are absent from Ireland and Scotland, Yorkshire being the most northerly county where they are found. The Ouse and its tributaries are well populated. Many of the Irish and Scottish game rivers, being clear, fast and gravelly, would be perfectly suited to the species, which has thrived extremely well since being introduced into Wales and the upper reaches of the River Wye. Old Father Thames and its tributaries, the Lea, the Wey, Kennet, Windrush and Evenlode, is justly famous for its stock of barbel. And its sister river, the Great Ouse, contains in its upper and middle reaches far greater populations than most anglers realize.

The most famous barbel rivers are the Dorset Stour and the Hampshire Avon, where the British record of 14 lb 6 oz was caught from the Royalty fishery at Christchurch by Mr A. D. Tryon in 1934. The Hampshire Avon also produced a monster barbel of 16 lb 1 oz to a salmon fisherman during the closed season, which was not eligible for record status.

During the last 30 years, barbel have been successfully introduced into several English river systems where they were not previously found, and in most cases they now provide exciting action in addition to the indigenous species of that river. By far and away the most successful stocking was the introduction of barbel into the River Severn during the mid 1950s. Even some of its tributaries, the River Teme in particular, have now become fabulous barbel fisheries throughout their length. Small fish from the Severn are used to stock other rivers, and the Wensum is one river to have benefitted.

Barbel are also common to river systems throughout Europe. One of the most prolific barbel rivers I have ever fished is the River Ebro in Spain, which contains tremendous stocks of both carp and barbel. Ebro barbel look very similar to British barbel and bite with equal boldness, but their snouts appear less conical and their colouration is much drabber. I would hazard a guess that they are a subspecies of the barbel caught in Britain. Ebro barbel are also extremely willing to accept baits trotted only a couple of

The only two species
that might be confused
with a baby barbel are
gudgeon and stone
loach. However, baby
barbel are not caught
on rod and line very
frequently.

Viva Espana. John
hoists a barbel (a
similar species to the
British one) from the
prolific River Ebro,
which enters the
Mediterranean via
Spain's eastern
coastline 150 miles
south of Barcelona.

feet below the surface in 10 to 20 ft of fast water, and can even be seen foraging along the surface.

This could have something to do with the noticeably higher temperature at which the Ebro flows. Then again, a fish called 'pink carp' that I have caught in India when mahseer fishing, and which to all intents and purposes is a barbel, also comes from a river that flows at over 80° throughout the summer, yet it still only feeds on the bottom.

The mahseer itself (*Barbus tor*) is, of course, none other than a barbel. Despite its large scales and carp-like shape, the natural characteristics and preferences of this legendary Indian fish are exactly that of the barbel, from the sudden, arm-wrenching bite, when the hook is pulled home by the fish's own weight and panic, to the arduous bottom hugging fight which follows. Various types of barbel occur throughout the continent of Africa, and also in the USA, where they are given the undignified name of suckers.

The distribution of barbel types is very wide indeed. Andy Davison considers the resemblance between this 'pink carp', which lives in the warm and fast-flowing Indian rivers, and European barbel.

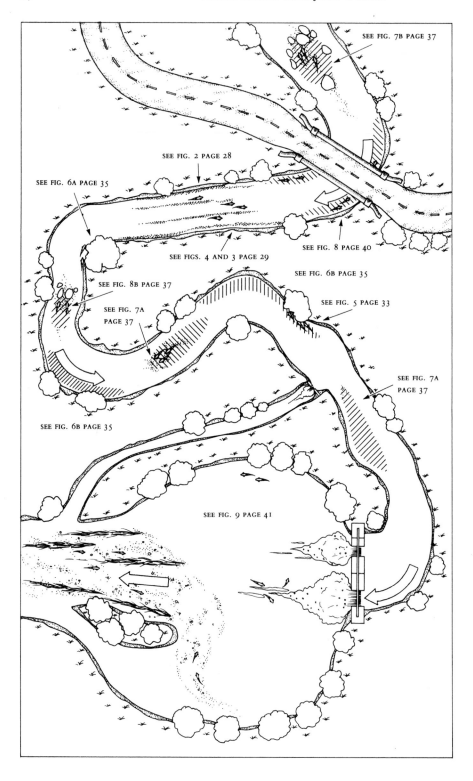

SEE FIG. 7B PAGE 37

SEE FIG. 2 PAGE 28

SEE FIG. 6A PAGE 35

SEE FIG. 8 PAGE 40

SEE FIGS. 4 AND 3 PAGE 29

SEE FIG. 6B PAGE 35

SEE FIG. 8B PAGE 37

SEE FIG. 5 PAGE 33

SEE FIG. 7A
PAGE 37

SEE FIG. 7A
PAGE 37

SEE FIG. 6B PAGE 35

SEE FIG. 9 PAGE 41

CHAPTER THREE

LOCATING BARBEL

BARBEL show an affinity with both chub and carp for choosing homes where they feel safe, with cover over their heads or at least close by. And if there is adjacent quiet water where they can rest away from the full force of the current, so much the better. They invariably prefer a clean bottom of well-scoured silt, sand or gravel, where the flow brings along a regular supply of natural food particles in addition to those found within the bottom strata and among the roots of nearby weeds, reeds and rushes.

Jungle-type swims among dense beds of flowering weeds or beneath lines of trees whose lower limbs are part sunken are especially suited to barbel, and for a reason that is not always immediately apparent to the fish-spotter above the surface. It is the increased current velocity caused by the river being channelled through narrow runs between dense vegetation, through gaps in an uneven bottom contour, between bridge arches and so on, that attracts the barbel.

Fortunately, in all but the deepest and widest rivers, barbel can be located visually in clear water during the summer months. And even if they are not given immediate attention, close studies of the depth and characteristics of each swim should be made, and the features mentally noted for later consideration.

There is a catch to all this observation, however, so be warned. Barbel-watching can become a fascinating but contagious disease for which there is no cure. You spend far more time stuck uncomfortably up a tree feeding and studying them than you do fishing for them. However, a useful spin-off is that you also learn to recognize the very

FIGURE 1 *Small to medium river, showing barbel swims in autumn*

Polaroid sunglasses, and the ability to climb the occasional tree in order to study your quarry and its environment during clear water conditions, are prerequisites for coming to grips with barbel on a regular basis in the smaller rivers.

definite features of barbel swims and habitats in other rivers where, through either excessive depth or water colour, the fish themselves cannot be seen. Remember, if you cannot find them, you certainly won't catch them.

Working tools of the trade for barbel location, in order of priority, start off with a good pair of scratch-resistant polaroid sunglasses, the importance of which cannot be over-stressed. A large proportion of anglers do not bother to buy the correct glasses for their particular requirements. They will happily pay over the top for designer rods and fancy reels, tackle gimmicks and the very latest in bait additives, but baulk at the suggestion that they purchase two pairs of good-quality polaroids with different coloured lenses. Nevertheless, that is what you should do.

For close observation of the river-bed in low light conditions, at dusk, dawn and during heavily overcast weather, I find the increased brightness provided by yellow lenses a real boon, with standard grey or amber lenses for use during bright, middle-of-the-day sessions.

For general observation of the river's contours and flow patterns, and for distant swims, it goes without saying that

Find the tall, green, onion-like stems of the true bullrush growing in sizeable clumps among channels of fast, bubbly water or smooth glides, and you have located barbel.

a pair of lightweight binoculars are also indispensible. Ideal sizes are 8 × 30 or 10 × 40 magnification.

Lightweight, thigh-length waders are also indispensible for reaching swims that can only be fished effectively by wading, and for climbing in to extract a heavily weeded fish every so often. Those with material-type uppers are preferable as they do not become uncomfortable when walking long distances. I also consider money on a pair of supple, lightweight chest-waders equally well spent. They enable you to reach those inaccessible spots in the middle of the river, and to use float tackle to explore tempting runs between long, flowing weed-beds. In addition, they let you reach impenetrable or snaggy swims on the opposite bank, where thick weedbeds between you and the barbel rule out bank fishing. After all, there is no point in hooking a barbel from a swim where you have no chance of extracting it. And during the summer months, when aquatic vegetation in some rivers is at its most rampant, a good half of the potentially productive barbel swims might instantly be out of bounds if you only ever consider bank fishing.

Having mentioned a few pointers, and the required equipment for locating this fascinating fish, let me now appraise a selection of natural (and man-made) features where the barbel is most likely to be found, given that the river you intend fishing has a reasonably prolific stock of fish.

BULLRUSHES

FIGURE 2 *Barbel occupy gravel and sand runs in corridors between clumps of bullrushes*

The true bullrush only grows in a firm, gravel bottom, and its tall, tapering, onion-like, blue-green stems grace the surface of the river in irregular-shaped clumps or beds, slightly bowed and gently quivering in the pull of the current. Bullrushes line the shallows in depths up to 3 ft and colonize shallow bars, even in the middle of the river-bed, and sometimes in huge clumps.

Above all others, this plant attracts barbel like bees to the proverbial honey-pot. The barbel feed on snails and eggs, plus a whole host of aquatic insect larvae that adhere to the base of the tough, perfectly round stems and upon the harvest of freshwater shrimps that scurry from one patch of stems to another.

Bullrush stems provide an interesting network of corridors and passageways along the bottom, with clean gravel or sandy runs between them – the perfect barbel habitat, providing sanctuary from harsh light and bankside disturbances, and with a readily available larder of food on tap (see fig. 2). So whenever you find bullrushes, even if only a few isolated patches in a river where they do not commonly grow, expect to find barbel. Even during the

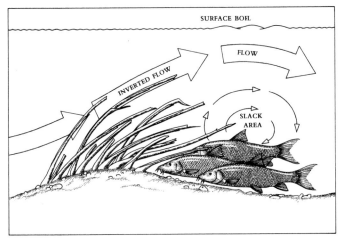

FIGURE 3 *When the river is in full flood barbel shelter behind the stumps of old bullrushes*

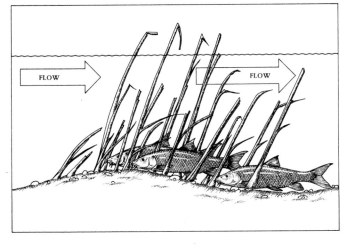

FIGURE 4 *Winter barbel worm their wiry bodies between dead and decaying bullrush stems when the river is cold and running low and clear*

During the winter months, bullrushes turn brown before rotting away, and in low, clear water conditions barbel love to work their way in between the irregularly shaped clumps.

winter months, when all that can be seen is a few broken stems protruding from just above the surface, barbel will not be far away. During flood time they gather behind what is left of the previous year's bullrush stumps for protection out of the main flow (see fig. 3). When the river runs cold, low and clear, providing little else in the way of natural cover, barbel worm their wiry bodies right in between the dead and decaying stems (fig. 4), venturing out into open water only during low light conditions and at night, and occasionally for the thoughtful fisherman who introduces a regular stream of loose feed such as casters, maggots or worm fragments, from a position a long way upstream so as not to alarm them.

MARGINAL PLANT COVER

Wherever sand or gravel runs along the margins are sufficiently shaded by lines of reed grass, common reed, tall sedges, watercress beds and the like covered with a

minimum depth of about 2 ft of water moving at a fair lick, barbel can be expected. Those runs where watercress or the floating stems of sweet reed grass hang out and form a canopy over part of the run, especially in mini slacks behind the heads of runs, are particularly inviting to barbel and angler alike. Deep runs with slacks close in are particularly suited to floatfishing with the bait anchored to the bottom (see Stret pegging, page 107).

Without question, the most beautiful of surface river plants is the water crowfoot, which sprouts from the gravel bottom in long wavering beds, topped by erect, daisy-like white and yellow flowers. Barbel adore the clear runs between the weedbeds and the shade they provide.

LONG, WAVERING WEED-BEDS

By far the most beautiful of these barbel-attracting plants is the water crowfoot, one of several Ranunculacea that root in gravel to form thick, wavering beds of 30 ft long or more, topped at the surface with delicate, daisy-like white flowers sporting yellow centres. Along with potomogeton, which also grows in long, flowing beds with a mass of tough stems and bright green leaves, these plants provide wonderful overhead cover and a dark hideout for barbel hugging the river-bed below. Those who regularly fish-spot for barbel know only too well how one minute a clear run between flowing weedbeds appears to be completely empty, and the very next the current sways the tail end of the weed mass momentarily to one side, revealing beneath it the shapes of numerous barbel that are then covered again just as quickly. If you are not concentrating, such happenings can seem like a mirage.

RAFTS AND OVERHANGING TREES

Barbel feel comfortable spending the daylight hours in subdued light, and the overhanging branches of certain trees invariably play host to a shoal or two. Mature, low-spreading alders are always worth exploring, but by far the best barbel tree is the willow, whose lower limbs often become submerged and sprout a beard of red-brown fibrous roots. Over the years, flotsam and silt collect in the margins around the base of these sunken branches, forming a dark, impenetrable cavern beneath that is capable of housing a large group of resident barbel.

During the summer months when cut weed collects around the trailing edges of a willow, the holding capacity of the habitat could easily double, resulting in quite disproportionate-sized groups of barbel occupying an area little more than a few square yards.

There is a favourite River Wensum swim that I have fished for close on 20 years now, during which time the line of goat willows along the bank has slowly spread into one mass of tangled branches some 40 ft long. It holds barbel all year through, plus chub, the odd trout and even a big, double-figure pike. During the summer months, the barbel dominate the 6-ft wide, sandy run immediately below the trailing edge, where direct sunlight cannot penetrate. From the edge of the run, stretching across the river to the opposite bank, are wall-to-wall rooted weedbeds. Therefore the bait must be placed somewhere in the run beneath the overhang or the barbel will not even see it, let alone accept it.

Because of the crystal-clear water, fishing this swim has

been most educational in that I have spent countless hours watching the barbels' reaction to various baits, both on and off the hook. I have also scuba-dived the run, slowly working my way beneath the dense canopy from a point well downstream, so as not to frighten the occupants. I lay there holding on to the bottom in case the flow swept me downstream, with barbel all around. Some nudged under my belly between wetsuit and bottom, others mooched inquisitively around the strange intruder who had the audacity to occupy pole position on the grid.

During one fascinating dive, I lay there quietly for a good 30 minutes, the giant among a group of no less than 22 barbel, ranging from 2 or 3 lb upwards to at least three specimens topping double figures. The experience even surpassed wanting to catch them. What I had not bargained for, however, was the sheer volume of water passing beneath the overhang, causing me to hang on to big flints among the sandy bottom, despite wearing 25 lb of lead weights around my waist.

FIGURE 5 *Typical tunnel overhang of sunken willow roots*

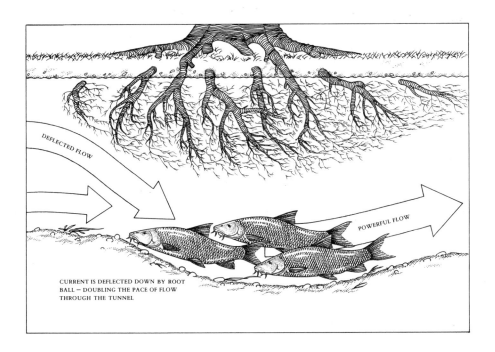

CURRENT IS DEFLECTED DOWN BY ROOT
BALL – DOUBLING THE PACE OF FLOW
THROUGH THE TUNNEL

The surface water was of course deflected downwards as it hit the willow branches, immediately doubling the flow through the tunnel – one of the reasons why barbel are so

Rafts of cut weed and debris that collect around the trailing branches of over-hanging willows are among the most prolific of all barbel habitats.

attracted to such habitats (see fig. 5). In fact, because of the volume of water being held back by dense beds of weed that spread across the river, the entire current force at this point of the river is channelled through tunnels where the barbel are lying.

An additional lesson that I learnt from playing footsies with fast-water barbel came from appreciating that I, too, could hold station close to the bottom provided that I kept my body angled slightly downwards (as opposed to horizontal). The force of the current does the rest with little additional physical effort required on the part of the diver.

Large trees, willow, ash, beech, alder and so on, which topple over into the river during gale-force winds or simply through old age, create potentially fine barbel swims until the river authority come along and remove them. So make hay while the sun shines, because like chub, barbel are quick off the mark in taking up residence among any entanglement of branches that appears along the bank, especially barbel living in rivers that are generally sparse in habitat features.

UNDERCUT BANKS

Beneath the roots of large willows and alders, and most especially on the outside of acute bends low down in the river, banking close to the bottom is liable to be undercut, providing habitat caverns much loved by barbel (see fig. 6).

Such features are invisible to the ardent fish-spotter,

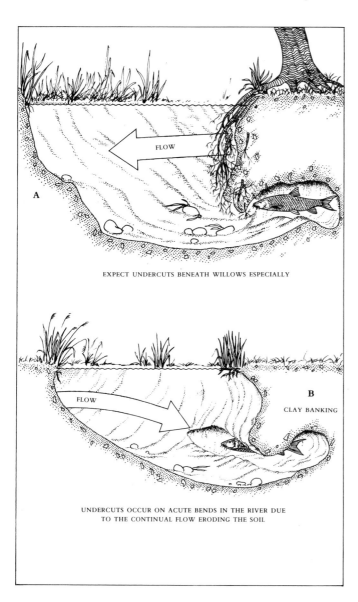

FIGURE 6 *Undercut banks are popular with barbel*

A

EXPECT UNDERCUTS BENEATH WILLOWS ESPECIALLY

FLOW

B

CLAY BANKING

UNDERCUTS OCCUR ON ACUTE BENDS IN THE RIVER DUE
TO THE CONTINUAL FLOW ERODING THE SOIL

even when the river is crystal clear. However, by kneeling down quietly on the very edge and looking straight down through polaroids to the bottom on the outside of an acute bend, you can usually see barbel slinking in and out, quite suddenly disappearing into the bank. On large, coloured rivers like the middle Great Ouse or Thames, where visibility makes such observation impossible, you can expect that somewhere beneath steep banking on the outside of most acute bends there will be an undercut and barbel will be present.

It is into these dark caverns that barbel retreat and spend a fair part of the day, resting with their heads stuck in a mass of roots, not even facing the flow. I have observed them beneath many undercuts, and also beneath tree lines in slacks close into the bank in a similar state, perhaps the closest to sleep as we know it.

In case you are thinking that Wilson only catches barbel because he plays with them beneath the surface, let me put the record straight. I never make a dive and afterwards start fishing. Scuba-diving is far too tiring a sport. Besides, my enquiring mind has for one day at least been totally satisfied by an hour-long diving sortie. The exact where-abouts of undercuts, and whether barbel inhabit the swim, are extremely useful pieces of information that I eventually might put to good use by visiting the same spots an hour before dark, when barbel are most liable to leave their cavern and forage. However, whether you believe me or not, in all honesty, most of the undercuts where I know barbel to exist, I have yet to fish.

DEPRESSIONS

In gravel-bottom and rocky rivers, where weeds are sparse and there is an almost complete lack of visible habitat features like marginal reeds, bullrushes, overhanging trees and the like, barbel occupy very definite bottom features. Natural depressions in the river-bed immediately down-stream of high spots or humps are choice swims, and barbel, like salmon and trout, love the quieter water immediately behind large boulders (see fig. 7).

Barbel are not so easy to see in fast, broken-water

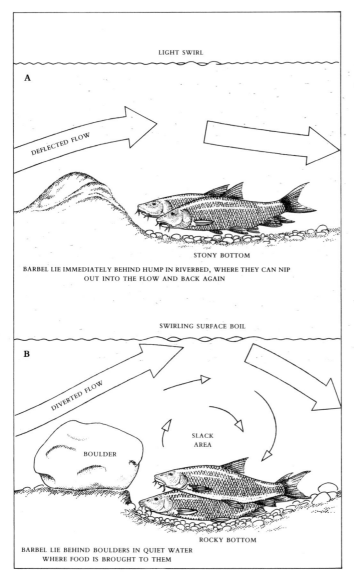

FIGURE 7 *Barbel lies in rocky rivers that are devoid of aquatic plants and marginal trees*

environments, especially where the bottom consists of many different coloured stones, because they blend in so well. I can well remember a lesson from fishing famous Throop Mill on the clear-flowing Dorset Stour many years ago, before the lower half of the fishery was altered for motorway construction. In those days, long stretches of the river-bed were very up and down, with long runs of gravel and different-coloured flints beneath much broken

A barbel haven, immediately below the famous railway bridge on the Hampshire Avon at the Royalty Fishery in Christchurch – a mixture of massive, flowing weedbeds and narrow, gravel runs where any clear depression is likely to contain barbel.

water only 3 to 4 ft deep, such was the current force, and it provided a wonderful barbel environment.

Much of the Stour contained lush, dense clumps of bullrush and wavering bright green weedbeds, like the classic barbel river it is. However, I became particularly fascinated by these long, broken-water runs and spent an entire 2-week vacation in pursuit of the occupants.

From a high bank immediately above the river, initial observation suggested the bottom was bare. All I could see through polaroid glasses was the occasional carrot-coloured stone among the freckled mass of rocks and gravel. After standing there for a minute or so, one of the carrot-coloured stones suddenly moved a few inches *upstream*.

It was, of course, the pectoral fin of a barbel, and once my eyes had become well and truly accustomed, focussed perfectly on the layer of water immediately above the bottom, which slowly happens only after several minutes of concentration, the physical forms of the barbel themselves started to become plainly visible. I was standing there above an enormous shoal of barbel, in a swim that everyone walked past, containing perhaps 40 fish or more.

It was impossible to count them accurately through the broken surface because they were in fact moving about and continually changing position, though extremely slowly.

After a good half an hour of concentrating my eyes upon the same long run, just about everything in the swim was now plainly visible to me. Interspersed between the barbel were a few small seatrout, and at the very top of the run close in to the bank lay a majestic salmon of at least 20 lb. How could I not have seen them all at first glance. There is indeed more to fish-spotting than meets the eye.

Bridges invariably create hot-spots, providing subdued light and an area of slack water immediately behind the centre supports. Barbel love to lie in wait here for the food particles delivered to them by the current.

BRIDGES

Not all bridges that cross the river attract barbel beneath them. Much depends on the formation of the river-bed both up and down stream, the angle of the main flow to the bridge, the depth beneath and, of course, the construction of the bridge itself. Those resting on steel or concrete pillars, for instance, are likely to support at least a small group of barbel, which shelter behind the pillars and in the undercuts eroded by the continual force of the water pushing against the concrete footings.

Where the river narrows to pass beneath a bridge, this in itself creates a faster push of water and thus will attract barbel. Ancient brick road-bridges spanning wide rivers are more liable to attract barbel than modern constructions. This is because time will have eroded the brickwork at river-bed level and created the odd undercut.

Bridges that are very low to the water, guaranteeing subdued light, even during the brightness of a summer's day, are by far the most productive barbel swims I have ever fished. The occupants of such a swim are willing to feed at any time.

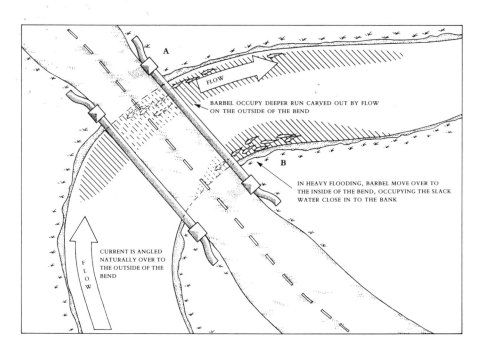

FIGURE 8 *Bridges over bends are best*

Bridges spanning the river on a bend are well worth exploring, as fig. 8A illustrates. A deeper run is always dug out on the outside of the bend beneath the bridge by the force of the current, and this is where the barbel will be lying. Such swims also produce during times of heavy flooding because the barbel move across to occupy the slacker water on the inside of the bend (fig. 8B) close in to the bank.

MILL AND WEIR POOLS

Of all the barbel-attracting habitats, weir-pools (and I use this word to cover both mill and weir pools because both have sluice gates) are the absolute tops. The mysterious, ever-changing pattern of surface currents is your visual guide to where barbel are lying below, bellies pressed close to the bottom. So take time to study the current direction

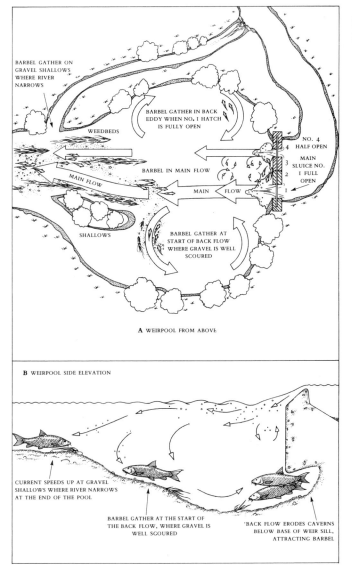

FIGURE 9 *Barbel location in weir-pools*

BARBEL GATHER ON GRAVEL SHALLOWS WHERE RIVER NARROWS

BARBEL GATHER IN BACK EDDY WHEN NO. I HATCH IS FULLY OPEN

WEEDBEDS

NO. 4 HALF OPEN

MAIN SLUICE NO. I FULL OPEN

BARBEL IN MAIN FLOW

MAIN FLOW

MAIN FLOW

SHALLOWS

BARBEL GATHER AT START OF BACK FLOW WHERE GRAVEL IS WELL SCOURED

A WEIRPOOL FROM ABOVE

B WEIRPOOL SIDE ELEVATION

CURRENT SPEEDS UP AT GRAVEL SHALLOWS WHERE RIVER NARROWS AT THE END OF THE POOL

BARBEL GATHER AT THE START OF THE BACK FLOW, WHERE GRAVEL IS WELL SCOURED

BACK FLOW ERODES CAVERNS BELOW BASE OF WEIR SILL, ATTRACTING BARBEL

carefully, looking in particular for runs of fast but steady water. Then use a heavy plummet to acquire an outline of the pool's bottom contours and its make up – gravel, silt, weedbeds, and so on.

In the summer months, especially during low water levels, the shallow bars, deep holes or runs and weedbeds are usually plainly obvious when you look through polaroid glasses. In some pools it is even possible to pinpoint visually groups of barbel hugging the fast, gravelly runs at the tail end of each flush. They love that extra pace of the water, which roach or bream, for instance, do not. They will move deeper into the pool once winter arrives, of course, but summer observation fixes so many pieces of the jigsaw together and stands you in good stead when the river runs coloured and these natural features cannot be seen. As all weir-pools are different in size, shape, depth and positioning of the operative sluices, each has its own-very special and definite character. Consider the weir-pool in fig. 9A, for instance, which has two sluices running (no. 1 is the more powerful) throughout the year, except in flood conditions when more gates are lifted to accommodate the extra push of water. Note from the side elevation (fig. 9B) how the current flows back towards the base of the weir sill, where caverns have been eroded away. Barbel love to occupy such spots and may be taken with a bait dropped straight down through the white water to the bottom layer, which flows in the opposite direction.

CHAPTER FOUR

TACKLE

A S barbel live in fast water for much of the time, they are the one species that always provide an exciting, powerful scrap, and while match fishermen do hook and even land them on fine hook lengths, superlight tackle plays no part in my barbel fishing. I prefer to play them on adequate, balanced tackle that provides an exhilarating fight in which the barbel is beaten but not totally exhausted.

The all-through, forgiving action of the Avon-style quivertip rod allows you to steer even large barbel hooked at close quarters away from snags. Having caught numerous specimens from his local River Wensum, Chris Shortis of Costessey, Norfolk, does not play barbel lightly. Neither does he lose many.

RODS

Ledger rods

The most useful barbel rod for both bomb and feeder fishing, and it would be my choice were I limited to just one, is the quivertip ledger. It is available in models ranging from 10 to 12 ft with spliced-in tips, to the multi-tips, which offer the choice of two or three different tips stored in the handle that push into the top joint; or a standard ledger rod with a threaded end-ring into which a quivertip is then screwed (see Quivertips, page 60).

My personal preference is for a 24 in fast-taper, solid glass tip built into an Avon-action, two-piece, 11–12 ft lightweight carbon fibre blank of around 1¼ lb test curve, which provides extreme sensitivity at the important end, yet power in reserve in the lower half beneath the forearm. Such rods deal comfortably with reel lines up to 6 lb test, yet permit hook lengths down to just 2 lb for modest-sized barbel in difficult, clear-water conditions.

For tackling barbel in the deep and heavy water of large rivers such as the Severn and Trent, a more powerful rod is advisable because the flow alone will bend a lighter rod over in the rest, thus rendering its spliced-in quivertip useless. Manufacturers that specialize in quivertip rods suitable for the rigours of barbel fishing are Ryobi, Daiwa and Silstar.

Those who enjoy constructing their own specialist rods will find a carbon carp blank of around 1½–1¾ lb test curve the perfect tool. Cut it back by 24 in at the top and splice in a 24 in solid-glass tip. The best tips are arrived at by cutting back a 3 ft solid glass, rapid-taper donkey top from the thick end (and a little off the fine tip if you wish) until it protrudes from the top of the cut blank, leaving just 2 in inside, which alleviates any chance of a 'dead spot' (see fig. 10).

Gently file the end of the top joint after carefully removing the last 24 in with a fine-tooth hacksaw, and instead of gluing in the quivertip, simply pull it through slowly with a degree of firmness and turn gently until it 'locks'. Do not be over forceful or you will split the carbon blank. Once the joint has been whipped over, there is no

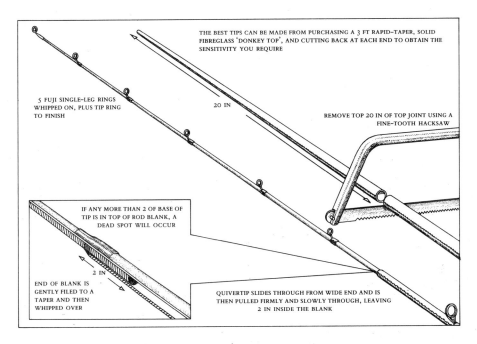

THE BEST TIPS CAN BE MADE FROM PURCHASING A 3 FT RAPID–TAPER, SOLID FIBREGLASS 'DONKEY TOP', AND CUTTING BACK AT EACH END TO OBTAIN THE SENSITIVITY YOU REQUIRE

5 FUJI SINGLE-LEG RINGS WHIPPED ON, PLUS TIP RING TO FINISH

20 IN

REMOVE TOP 20 IN OF TOP JOINT USING A FINE-TOOTH HACKSAW

IF ANY MORE THAN 2 OF BASE OF TIP IS IN TOP OF ROD BLANK, A DEAD SPOT WILL OCCUR

2 IN

END OF BLANK IS GENTLY FILED TO A TAPER AND THEN WHIPPED OVER

QUIVERTIP SLIDES THROUGH FROM WIDE END AND IS THEN PULLED FIRMLY AND SLOWLY THROUGH, LEAVING 2 IN INSIDE THE BLANK

FIGURE 10 *Sleeving solid-glass quivertip into top joint of carbon 2 pc powerful Avon-style rod blank*

chance of it slipping back down. Should you break the end of the fine tip at any time in the future (easily done), a replacement is easily sleeved in. To remove the broken tip, undo the whipping and hold the quivertip tightly. Gently knock the base of the top joint against a stone or wooden floor until it slides down inside the joint and can be pulled through.

To complete, whip on five or six small, one-leg, fuji, lined rings plus a tip and paint the last 20 in with two coats of matt white paint. This really makes it stand out, so even tiny bites are easily seen in poor light conditions, whatever the background.

Ledger/float rods

The standard 11–12 ft two-piece, carbon Avon rod is an extremely useful addition to the barbel fisherman's armoury. Even without the quivertip in its 1¼ lb test curve, the tip of most models are fine enough for rod-top ledgering considering that on most occasions barbel do bite boldly, and for most floatfishing requirements the rod is perfect.

The most versatile rods of all are those designed with

A 13-ft, reasonably meaty waggler rod coupled to a centre-pin reel is the ideal outfit for enjoying the fight of modest-sized barbel while long-trotting.

two tips, such as the Ryobi Avon carbon quivertip, which has a standard 1¼ lb test curve top plus a built-in quivertip top joint. Thus, the one unit handles all eventualities from quivertip ledgering to stret pegging or long trotting, and reel lines from 3 to 6 lb test.

Trotting rods

As I have already mentioned, the standard Avon rod of 11 ft or 12 ft nicely covers most floatfishing requirements. However, there are times when long trotting on medium-paced water for modest-sized barbel permits the use of a longer, lightweight float rod. To maximize on line pick up and for better float control, my preference is for a 13 ft, reasonably meaty waggler rod in carbon fibre that has either a fairly thick wall or a wrapping of shock-absorbing strengthener like 'Kevlar'. I am then perfectly happy trotting with lines up to 5 lb test and bending the rod fully into barbel. Most general-purpose, super-light, match-style float rods are not up to the kind of punishment that

long trotting for barbel can impart, so beware. Choose that float rod very carefully.

A silky-smooth clutch adjusted exactly to the line test being used helps enormously when you are trying to extract barbel from jungle swims, because you can give only the minimum of line.

REELS

Fixed-spool reels

A small to medium format fixed-spool reel in the 2000–2500 size is the ideal choice for ledgering, and doubles nicely for stret pegging or even long trotting if you are not a centre-pin enthusiast. I recommend a smooth-running (ball-bearing) model that has a roller in the bale arm to reduce friction and possible line fracture when the barbel characteristically belts off down river, ripping line fast from the spool. A silky smooth slipping clutch is imperative. It does not matter whether the clutch adjustment is on the spool itself or at the rear in the form of a calibrated drag knob. The important point is its 'smoothness', because I prefer to fish with the anti-reverse permanently on and the clutch adjusted to the strength of the line, rather than back-winding, which invariably allows the barbel more line that is necessary – not a healthy exercise, especially when fishing close to snags or between dense weedbeds. Spools loaded to the brim with 5 and 6 lb line for ledgering and 3, 4 or 5 lb for floatfishing should cover most situations. When faced with the necessity of placing the bait into real jungle swims or in exceptionally heavy water, however, it is comforting to have an extra spool loaded with 7 or even 8 lb test in the tackle bag.

Centre-pin reels

That centre-pins are technically far superior to both the fixed-spool and closed-face reels for long trotting is beyond question. Nothing can compete with the way in which a float can be used to 'ease' the bait slowly downstream along the river-bed with the line in a straight line from float to rod tip, in complete readiness for an instant strike. And no other reel can match that pleasurable, direct feeling of playing a barbel with your thumb pressure gently braking the edge of the drum, ready to give line instantly should the fish suddenly charge off.

In all except the widest of barbel rivers the centre-pin is a lovely reel to use, whether trotting or stret pegging. I have in regular use both the Adcock Stanton, which runs super-smoothly on a ball-bearing race for over a minute to the slightest tap, and an ancient, original Match Aerial. Fortunately the latter is once again being produced in limited numbers after being unobtainable for many years, so while good centre-pins are certainly not cheap the would-be enthusiast is well catered for.

Making a line guard

A point worth mentioning about centre-pins is that unless you fit them with a line guard, you will experience all sorts of problems. During really windy weather, for instance, you will forever be looking down to free line that is flapping behind the cage, and this means that you lose concentration and take your eyes off the float.

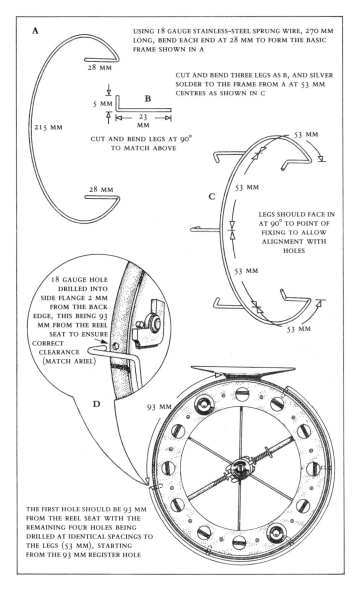

FIGURE 11 *Making a line guard*

A

USING 18 GAUGE STAINLESS-STEEL SPRUNG WIRE, 270 MM LONG, BEND EACH END AT 28 MM TO FORM THE BASIC FRAME SHOWN IN A

28 MM

CUT AND BEND THREE LEGS AS B, AND SILVER SOLDER TO THE FRAME FROM A AT 53 MM CENTRES AS SHOWN IN C

B
5 MM
23 MM

215 MM

CUT AND BEND LEGS AT 90° TO MATCH ABOVE

53 MM

28 MM

C   53 MM

LEGS SHOULD FACE IN AT 90° TO POINT OF FIXING TO ALLOW ALIGNMENT WITH HOLES

53 MM

18 GAUGE HOLE DRILLED INTO SIDE FLANGE 2 MM FROM THE BACK EDGE, THIS BEING 93 MM FROM THE REEL SEAT TO ENSURE CORRECT CLEARANCE (MATCH ARIEL)

53 MM

D   93 MM

THE FIRST HOLE SHOULD BE 93 MM FROM THE REEL SEAT WITH THE REMAINING FOUR HOLES BEING DRILLED AT IDENTICAL SPACINGS TO THE LEGS (53 MM), STARTING FROM THE 93 MM REGISTER HOLE

It is easy to construct an extremely efficient cage-type line guard, the design of which fits both reels previously mentioned perfectly. As you can see from fig. 11A, it is made from 18 gauge stainless-steel sprung wire (the sort tackle shops sell for making-up wire sea-booms), and can be adapted to fit virtually any make of centre-pin reel, although originally I designed it to fit the Match Aerial.

Start by shaping the wire into slightly more than a half circle fractionally larger than the diameter of the spool or

It is almost impossible to long trot effectively for barbel (or any other fish) unless your centre-pin reel is fitted with a line guard. Ray Page carefully unhooks a River Lea barbel that fancied maggots.

drum, with 1½ in ends bent back at right angles, as in fig. 11B.

To form cross-bars, four 1½ in lengths of the same wire are then silver-soldered neatly to the guard, as in fig. 11B. This is a task that most small engineering firms will do for a small charge. Insist that all solder joints are really smooth or the line will chafe on them. The ends of all six bars are then bent inwards at right angles (fig. 11C) and clipped off with wire cutters to 5/16 in long for fixing into the side flange of the reel's back plate once you have drilled holes to accommodate them (fig. 11D).

This job must be done accurately because the tolerance between back plate and spool is minimal, though more than enough for an 18 gauge hole to be drilled without the wire ends fouling the back of the spool. This job can be farmed out, and the local jewellers shop is the place to go.

Provided that all goes well and the guard has been carefully made, being a half-circle of sprung wire it clips neatly into the holes and holds itself firmly in place.

LINES

I like a supple, reasonably stretchy monofilament for barbel fishing in the hope that all sudden lunges made by the fish's powerful tail will be subdued by the inherent elasticity. Brands like Sylcast, Bayer Perlon and Maxima, which I have used for many years, seem to possess just the right amount of stretch for my taste and for the way I fish, which, to be fair, friends say is rather heavy-handed.

I would caution you against using a low-diameter, low-stretch brand, most of which have insufficient elasticity as a reel line for general barbel fishing. In special circumstances, it can be beneficial to use a finer diameter line as a hook length to encourage more bites in swims where there is plenty of room to enjoy an unhurried scrap. However,

A stretchy reel line and Avon-style rod allows John to extract a good barbel from a tangle of tree roots and trailing branches, despite his seemingly heavy-handed approach.

you must then take great care when the barbel is on a short line beneath the rod tip and has enough strength left for a last attempt at diving back down to the bottom again – a fairly common occurrence. Remember to loosen the drag knob on the reel's slipping clutch as the fish nears the net.

For ledgering with both bomb and feeder in fast rivers full of snags, overhanging trees, heavy weedbeds, and so on, I regard a 6 lb reel line as standard, stepping down to a 5 lb or even 4 lb hook link as conditions and circumstances permit. A common situation that arises in clear water during the summer and autumn is that barbel refuse the bait offered on a hook length of the strength required to extract them, but bite readily on a much finer hook length.

This problem is not always solved by stepping down if by doing so you are incapable (on such a light hook length) of stopping the barbel from reaching the sanctuary of snags. And we are not necessarily talking about big barbel here. Fish of just 2 and 3 lb can show an amazing turn of speed and power over a few yards. So my advice is always to ere on the heavier side with lines rather than lighter. Finicky barbel can be persuaded to accept a hook length of the necessary strength either by fishing after dark when they are less wary because they cannot see the line so well, or by presenting the bait on a hair rig (see Hair rig presentation, page 89). For tackling modest-sized fish in relatively snag-free conditions and also when winter fishing, I generally step down to a 5 lb reel line for ledgering and a 4 lb reel line for floatfishing with hooks tied direct. Then again, in really clear water, a reduction in hook-length strength can produce far more bites.

Another way of encouraging more bites is to use a soft dacron hook length which, being more supple than monofilament, permits a more natural presentation of the bait. There are various makes of braided hook-length (dacron types) material from which to choose, in flecked green, brown or plain black. Those made by Drennan, Ryobi, Kryston, and Black Spider are particularly recommended (see Hair rig presentation, page 89). It must be pointed out, however, that as synthetic hook lengths are non-stretch, the elasticity of the terminal rig is effectively reduced when a barbel is held beneath the rod tip on a short line immediately prior to netting. So slack off on the clutch and take great care.

HOOKS

Barbel fishing demands a really strong, sharp hook in the smaller sizes, and the Drennan forged, eyed, carbon, super-specialist hook in sizes 12 down to 20 fits the bill perfectly. These chemically-etched hooks are unusually strong for their size, and can be confidently tied on lines that are considerably heavier than you would trust other hook patterns with. For instance, a single corn kernel on a size 12 tied direct to 4 lb or even 5 lb test is quite in order, as is, say, a single caster on an 18 or 20 tied direct to 2 lb test. I also use this pattern with complete confidence when fishing among snags or dense weed and presenting larger offerings: sizes 4 and 6 for whole prawns and cockles or small dead fish, cheese paste, worms and so on; and sizes 8 and 10 for crust cubes and flake, luncheon meat cubes, tares, corn or maize presented two or three up, and so on.

In clear water conditions when there is reasonable room for playing barbel without having to exert extreme pressure, I like to use the Drennan forged, round-bend, carbon, specimen, eyed hook, which is still incredibly strong, but a noticeably 'lighter' hook. It provides a more delicate presentation of the bait, especially in the smaller sizes from 10 down to 16.

As I only ever fish with eyed hooks for barbel (and carp for that matter), there is little point in my recommending spade-end patterns.

KNOTS

In my experience the strongest, most reliable knot for tying on eyed hooks is the mahseer knot. After all, if it's good enough to match the world's largest barbel, the Indian mahseer, then it is certainly good enough for the mahseer's British counterpart. The beauty of this knot, apart from the fact that it stretches under a full load without strangling the line, is that it cannot come undone, because the end is trapped beneath two coils, as in clinch knots, yet it is as easy and quick to tie as a blood knot (see fig. 12A). Unfortunately, because the eyes of modern,

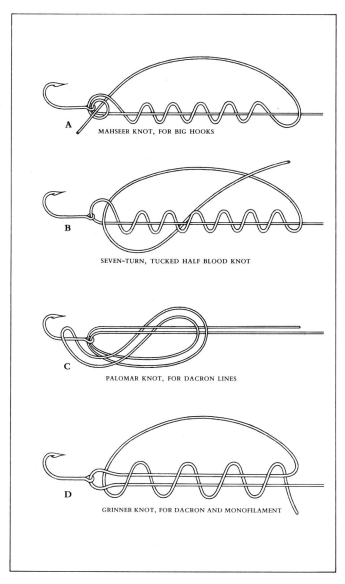

A MAHSEER KNOT, FOR BIG HOOKS

B SEVEN-TURN, TUCKED HALF BLOOD KNOT

C PALOMAR KNOT, FOR DACRON LINES

D GRINNER KNOT, FOR DACRON AND MONOFILAMENT

Opposite *You need forged hooks when barbel fishing, and a pair of long-nosed artery forceps to remove the hook from the barbel's thick, rubbery lips.*

FIGURE 12 *Knots*

chemically etched hooks are extremely small, and because the line needs to pass twice through the eye, it is not always possible to use the mahseer knot. I then opt for the seven-turn, 'tucked' half blood knot in fig. 12B, which is a reliable second choice. Remember with all knots to wet them with saliva before pulling tight. The hook will then hang nicely and the last inch of line will not crimp or curl.

For tying hooks and swivels to make a dacron hook link, the correct knot to use is the palomar (fig. 12C), which causes minimal strangulation of this synthetic line. The

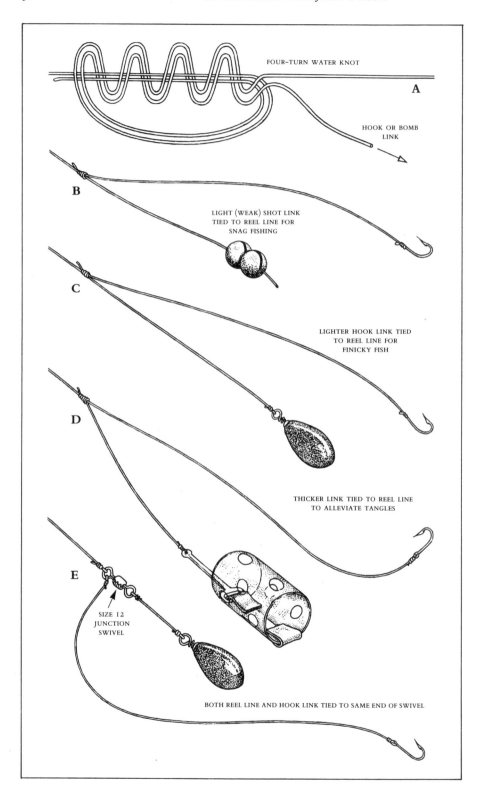

FOUR-TURN WATER KNOT

A

HOOK OR BOMB
LINK

B

LIGHT (WEAK) SHOT LINK
TIED TO REEL LINE FOR
SNAG FISHING

C

LIGHTER HOOK LINK TIED
TO REEL LINE FOR
FINICKY FISH

D

THICKER LINK TIED TO REEL LINE
TO ALLEVIATE TANGLES

E

SIZE 12
JUNCTION
SWIVEL

BOTH REEL LINE AND HOOK LINK TIED TO SAME END OF SWIVEL

palomar can prove rather difficult to tie with certain eyed hooks because the doubled line will not pass through small, neat eyes. When this happens, use the grinner knot (fig. 12D), which again is far less constricting than the blood knot for dacron line. The grinner is also a most reliable knot to use with monofilament if you cannot manage the mahseer knot.

FIGURE 13 *End rigs and knots*

For joining 2–3 ft of slightly lighter (finer) hook length to the reel line for trotting with small baits, or for making a simple fixed paternoster ledger, consider the four-turn water knot (fig. 13A). This reliable, neat and easy knot allows you to tie a weak bomb or shot link (so it breaks when snag fishing) to the reel line (fig. 13B); or a lighter hook link to the reel line for a finer presentation to finicky fish (fig. 13C); or a thicker ledger or swimfeeder link to the reel line (fig. 13D), which stands away from the reel line and alleviates tangles.

As an alternative to the four-turn water knot, use a tiny size 12 swivel (fig. 13E) as the junction, remembering always to tie both hook link and reel line to the same end of the swivel. Then, if the swivel breaks in half you are still connected to the barbel.

FLOATS

Slim-tipped, super-sensitive floats play little part in trotting for barbel. You need something to carry a good shotting load in the fast water where barbel live, so that the bait is taken straight down to tumble along the bottom in the manner in which the current delivers all natural titbits to them.

For attractive bait presentation in smooth, medium-paced swims, a range of big sticks or balsa trotters carrying from 4 to 8 BB will do nicely. Where the current pace necessitates upwards of two swan shots, I use chubbers, Avons and the cork on crowquill specials made by Topper Haskins. Being rather squat with a thick, easy-to-see tip, and having a large shotting capacity of up to 5 swan shots, chubbers are the ideal float for really shallow, distant swims where a long float travelling continually over their heads might easily spook the barbel. By the same token,

During his exploits in India in search of the world's largest barbel, the legendary mahseer, John managed to bag in a single session this brace of monsters (one on paste, the other on a small deadbait) totalling over 170 lb, from currents going at incredible speed. His 6/0 hook was tied with the reliable mahseer knot shown on page 55.

for trotting the bait steadily downstream in deep, swirling water, a long float such as the Avon or cork on crowquill is the perfect tool for the job.

For stret pegging, where the float lies flat (see Stret pegging, page 107) on the surface once the bait has settled on the river-bed, I use a length of plain peacock-quill, balsa trotters or Avons.

While some of these floats come ready fitted with neat bottom rings, I nevertheless prefer to attach them at both the top and bottom with bands of silicon tubing. This achieves two purposes. It allows for a rapid changeover from one float to another, and it provides a safety margin in that should a barbel become weeded, the float will pop out of the bands instead of remaining on the line and possibly causing a break. You could lose a float yet land the barbel.

QUIVERTIPS

Made to fit all ledger rods with a threaded end-ring, screw-in quivertips are available in a range of test curves from 1 oz to 3½ oz to suit current strength and the taper of the rod. Ensure that the tip you choose will take on a slight bend under pressure from the current with enough flexibility in the tip to register a gentle knock without the fish feeling undue resistance. If it bends over completely, the tip is too light, so change to a stiffer one. In situations where both tip and top joint are bent right over in a full curve by extreme current pressure, dispense with the tip altogether and simply rely on watching the rod top for bites.

Many of the commercially produced screw-in quivertips are fitted only with the tiny tip ring and no intermediates. They can instantly be improved by whipping on a small single-leg ring halfway between the screw thread and the tip. The line will then follow the curvature of the tip when fully bent without any nasty angles. If you experience difficulty in concentrating on the narrow band of fluor-escent colour with which most quivertips are painted, give the entire tip two thick coats of matt white. It then really stands out against a variety of backgrounds, allowing you to determine the tiniest knocks even in poor light. If it is illuminated after dark with a narrow torch beam, it can be watched for many hours without causing eye strain.

SUNDRIES

Landing-nets

As barbel are regularly netted from swims with heavily overgrown weed beds or from snags in confined gaps between the bankside trees or tall rushes and reeds, an easily manoeuvrable, lightweight landing-net with a strong 9–10 ft telescopic handle is an absolute necessity. My preference is for a 24 in diameter round frame with a 24 in deep mixed-mesh net with soft, knotless minnow-mesh sides and a barbel-friendly micro-mesh base. Even large, specimen-sized barbel several inches longer than the net's width easily roll in and, due to the deep mesh, stand no chance of rolling out. If you prefer a triangle frame, go for a lightweight model with fibre glass, 30 in arms and a deep twin mesh.

Once a barbel has recovered in a keep-net and livened up again, finds weighing a difficult and stressful operation. Do not bother with specialized bags or slings. Lying quietly in the bottom of a soft landing-net after a spirited fight, the fish is in the perfect receptacle. Unscrew the net top from the pole and hook the frame directly on to the scales, remembering to deduct the net's weight after releasing the barbel.

RETAINING BARBEL

Unlike most species caught on rod and line, barbel really do give their all and battle doggedly until all their strength has been sapped. It is one of their most endearing characteristics, and a reason why I will not fish for them using ultra-light tackle. The longer they fight, the longer they could take to recover. Indeed, I doubt there is a barbel fisherman alive who has not got into the river to hold his

Because they carry a fair amount of shot to get the bait down quickly and keep it there for a steady search of the swim, these are the floats to use when trotting for barbel.

Opposite A round, 24-in diameter landing net frame fitted with a deep twin-mesh net is not only very manoeuvrable for netting barbel hooked in awkward, confined swims, it becomes the perfect receptacle, once unscrewed from the pole, for weighing them in.

prize upright for several minutes, head into the current so it can recover by absorbing a constant supply of dissolved oxygen.

After a while, the gills can be seen working strongly and a sense of power is felt beneath the hand grasping the narrow tail wrist. It is ready for return from whence it came. I can remember many years ago during a heatwave summer, when fishing the upper Thames at Farringdon, my brother Dave was committed to supporting a barbel upright for over an hour after the weighing in, much to the annoyance of fellow club members who sat in the coach ready to start the long journey back to north London. There was no way that Dave would allow that barbel to go back until it was fully recovered.

The point to remember, therefore, when you retain barbel, is never to cram them into a keep-net where they need to compete for a finite amount of dissolved oxygen. Invest in a wide, long, micro-mesh net – one around the dimensions of 20 in wide by 10 ft long will do nicely – and stake it out fully in water that is flowing strongly. Not, I repeat not, in the slack water close into the bank where margin growth invariably restricts the flow. Beware of introducing barbel, particularly small barbel, into nets with larger mesh than micro. Their serrated first dorsal spine all too easily catches in the mesh, with the result that they hang there like washing on the line when the net is removed from the river.

A particularly 'barbel-friendly' keep-net is manufactured by Keenets. It is called 'safe flo', and a soft black nylon material with punched holes covers the last two rings instead of micro-mesh netting. It creates a darker, less stressful environment compared to the standard keep-net, and is available in lengths up to 13 ft, and in 20 in diameter rings, or in a 20 x 16 in rectangular format.

A ruse for creating a darker, less stressful situation for barbel lying in a standard net placed in shallow, clear water during a bright summer day is to pull up a piece of weed (or a carp sack) and hang it over the entire length of the net – simple yet most effective. Never leave a barbel upside down inside the keep-net if it suddenly turns turtle. Hold its head directly into the fastest water you can stand in until its gills are working strongly, then release it straight away.

For retaining a single specimen barbel prior to photography, the tunnel or tubes manufactured by E. T. Fishing Tackle from soft nylon, through which the current flows via punched holes, are excellent. They take up nowhere near the room of a keep-net and so suit the travel-light style of the exploring barbel angler.

CHAPTER FIVE

BAITS

Barbel fishing during my teens centred mostly around the lovely old original course of the River Lea bordering Hertfordshire and Middlesex, between Wormly and Enfield Lock. Living close to this picturesque winding haven (much of which has now ceased to exist due to development of the Lea Valley Leisure Scheme) gave me the opportunity to catch numbers of small to modest-sized barbel on a variety of baits from breadcrust to elderberries and with some rather offbeat methods. I can well remember one unusual October afternoon with the river running low and exceptionally clear, when I accounted on freelined bread flake for no less than 22 small barbel plus a 3 lb chub, all from a tiny gap in an entanglement of thick willow branches beneath an overhang. This tiny swim was virtually static and barely 3 ft deep, but it was crammed with the entire stock of fish that, under normal river conditions, was spread out along the gravel run in fast, bubbly water in front of the overhang. As the run was now covered by mere inches of water, everything had taken refuge within the entanglement of sub-surface roots – the perfect hideout, or so they thought. Peering through polaroid glasses at the thumbnail pinch of bread flake covering an 8 hook and tied direct to 5 lb test, which sank slowly towards the bottom, I was treated to a wonderful sight. Long before it settled, a barbel would move upwards intercepting it aggressively in that distinct, agitated manner they have of moving their head quickly from side to side. And they kept coming one after another almost until the cupboard was bare.

I doubt that the fact I used bread flake, and here is the point of this particular story, resulted in so many barbel being extracted from that little spot. I am convinced that lobworms, corn, cheese paste, maggots, and so on would each have resulted in exactly the same haul. I used flake

because I could follow it visually all the way down to the bottom and because it sank slowly. The fact is, barbel can be caught on a far greater variety of baits than most anglers realize. What is more, the key to consistent success is to ring the changes and switch from one bait to another when the fish start to become wary of a particular bait.

NATURAL BAITS

Lobworms

Equipped with a torch and a gallon-sized plastic bucket strung around your neck, just an hour's evening jaunt around the local cricket pitch after a heavy downpour will provide you with enough barbel baits for several weeks.

Barbel are attracted to the distinct 'aroma' of animal baits, and especially those which wriggle like a big, juicy lobworm. Now I know it is an effort to leave the arms of a good woman, a Clint Eastwood film or a comfortable chair to set out in the dark for a bait-collecting jaunt, especially when a long walk or drive only takes you to the local cricket pitch (unless you have a large Wembley-type lawn in your back garden), but believe me, it is worth it.

There is nothing like a supply of fresh lobworms harvested from a sopping wet lawn, the secret being to watch the weather carefully and only set forth after a prolonged spell of rain. In a very short space of time, you will be able to stock up with enough lobworms to satisfy your needs for many weeks ahead.

When the ground is really wet and the rain has dwindled to just a fine spray, or stopped completely, lobworms are more likely to be out of their holes, lying there on top of the wet grass waiting to be picked up. There is no heavy pulling, no feverish tug-of-war with worms that, even if you manage to extract them, never amount to much and often die within a few days because they have been held too tightly.

The old-style barbel fishing once commonly practised on large rivers like the Thames and the Trent consisted of pre-baiting a favourite run, usually at the tail end of a weir-pool, with 1,000–2,000 lobworms every day for a week or so prior to fishing. No doubt such gross tactics would work today, though I fancy shoals in the larger rivers are now very much smaller, but who fancies collecting thousands upon thousands of lobs. Certainly not I. An

FIGURE 14 *Worms*

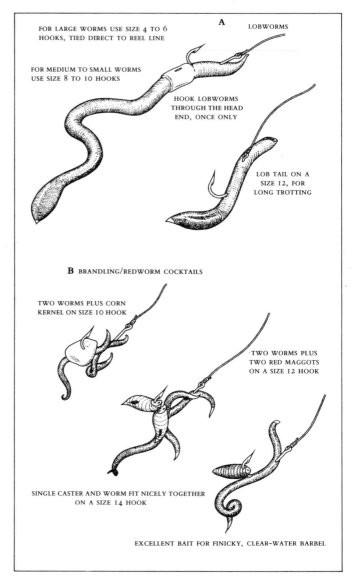

FOR LARGE WORMS USE SIZE 4 TO 6
HOOKS, TIED DIRECT TO REEL LINE

A   LOBWORMS

FOR MEDIUM TO SMALL WORMS
USE SIZE 8 TO 10 HOOKS

HOOK LOBWORMS
THROUGH THE HEAD
END, ONCE ONLY

LOB TAIL ON A
SIZE 12, FOR
LONG TROTTING

B BRANDLING/REDWORM COCKTAILS

TWO WORMS PLUS CORN
KERNEL ON SIZE 10 HOOK

·TWO WORMS PLUS
TWO RED MAGGOTS
ON A SIZE 12 HOOK

SINGLE CASTER AND WORM FIT NICELY TOGETHER
ON A SIZE 14 HOOK

EXCELLENT BAIT FOR FINICKY, CLEAR-WATER BARBEL

hour's worming on the local cricket pitch is about all my
back will stand. Incidentally, for those new to the art of
worm stalking, do not rush about with a quartz halogen
flashlight. Pick your feet up carefully as you walk slowly
along (just like a chicken does) and use a wide-beam torch
of medium power, otherwise every worm on the pitch will
be halfway down its hole before you bend down. Lastly, to
keep both hands free (one for the torch, the other for
picking up worms) hang a 1-gallon plastic bait bucket
around your neck at chest height.

Having tried presenting lobworms every which way over the years, I have come to the conclusion that hooking the worm once only through the head end is best (see fig. 14A). The worm can at least work naturally, and thus looks far more appealing to the barbel than if it is double hooked. And fewer bites are missed through the hook point doubling back into the worm instead of into the barbel's mouth.

Select hook sizes to match that of the lobworm. Huge snakes go best on size 4 or 6 hooks (tied direct to the reel line), while medium to small worms fit nicely on sizes 8 and 10. For long trotting, present a whole small lob on a size 10, or the tail end only on a size 12. Lawn lobs keep best if packed loosely in clumps of sphagnam moss in a large bait tin.

Brandlings and redworms

These, the larger the better, are also much loved by barbel, and work especially well as cocktail baits in conjunction with sweetcorn, maggots or casters (see fig. 14B). In clear, low water conditions a single brandling or redworm on a size 14 hook topped with a single caster is an irresistable offering to finicky barbel.

Maggots

Without question a bunch of lively maggots is one of the most effective barbel baits. The trouble is that most other fish, especially minnows and dace, young roach and chub, also like them. In rivers like the Hampshire Avon, small seatrout can also pose a problem during the warmer months. However, if you feed the swim with several pints of maggots for an hour or two to occupy unwanted species, you will give the barbel a chance of a much longer look at your hook bait. During this time you can happily wade through all the smaller species (and when long trotting between long, flowing weedbeds from a position in the middle of the river this can be fun) with the odd chance of a barbel. Or you could ledger a large, static bait while keeping a regular stream of maggots going into the

Where small fish do not become a nuisance, maggots are one of the prime baits for barbel, whether ledgered or long trotted.

swim every few minutes, switching over to a maggot hook bait once the nuisance fish are full up.

When barbel are really on to the maggots tumbling along the bottom, you can see a 'flash' of a long golden flank every so often as they twist along the river-bed, dislodging particles of food. When this occurs regularly, they are feeding confidently and bites can usually be expected.

Of course, when going for barbel in rivers where nuisance species do not exist, maggots are the top of the list of baits to try.

I have not experienced a situation where barbel show a preference for one particular colour of maggot over another, and I generally use plain, large whites. However, this is not to say that in hard-fished stretches of river the barbel will not on occasion respond more readily to either red or bronze. In really clear water conditions it is always worth experimenting if bites are not forthcoming and you can see barbel in the swim. Incidentally, when wading out to trot for barbel, a bait apron or pouch that belts around the waist dispenses with the need for cumbersome bait boxes that need to be opened and closed continually.

Casters

Of all the small baits, casters are second only to the magical powers of hempseed. It goes without saying that casters presented on the hook over a bed of hempseed is a deadly combination. Bunches of casters work well with eight or nine crammed on to a size 6 or 8 hook, as do a brace of casters gently weaved on to a size 14, and maggot and caster cocktails – worm and caster, crust and caster, even meat and caster. And when clear, slow-water barbel are particularly choosey, as they can be especially during the middle of the day, a single caster with a size 18 hook buried inside it will produce when all else fails.

Whether introduced by hand, catapulted, or in a swimfeeder, casters and sweetcorn are very high on John's list of top barbel baits.

Prawns and shrimps

These superb baits will catch barbel, whether cooked or uncooked and whether peeled or left in their skins. As barbel feed on freshwater shrimps and crayfish, they accept saltwater crustaceans with equal relish.

Prawns and shrimps can be ledgered just like a cube of meat or cheese paste, or trundled just above the river-bed beneath a float with fragments thrown into the head of the swim as loose-feed attractors. Salmon anglers regularly take barbel when presenting mounted prawns (and on ridiculously heavy tackle too). In fact, one of the largest authenticated barbel ever caught from British waters, weighing 16 lb 1 oz, came to a salmon fisherman using the prawn at Ibsley on the famous Hampshire Avon. Unfortunately, the monster was foul hooked and could not therefore be accepted as a record. However, its capture proves the effectiveness of prawns as a bait for barbel.

Prawns and shrimps are best purchased fresh from the fish market and should be bagged up quickly and popped into the freezer for future use. When boiled, they turn pink of course, and look very different from the translucent, grey-green of their natural state. They change yet again when peeled and ready for human consumption. However, the barbel is not fussy, and will gobble them up in any state. It is well to remember that when peeled, prawns and shrimps are quite soft and you should take care when hooking them on and when casting.

Cockles

Once boiled and removed from their hard shells, cockles are another sea bait that catch barbel. Looking every bit like the insides of a tiny freshwater mussel that barbel consume as part of their natural diet, it is small wonder that cockles are so effective.

Purchase cockles in bulk, ready boiled and shelled, from the fishmarket. Divide them into two batches, bag them up and pop them into the freezer. Two pints should be sufficient for a day's barbel fishing. Cockles can be dyed easily and effectively if you fancy a spot of experimenting. Add a teaspoon of powder (carp bait) dye to the same quantity of boiling water as you have cockles and swish them around in a bowl for a couple of minutes so they colour evenly. Leave for half an hour and drain off surplus water before bagging up and freezing. Pink, red and orange are colours worth trying. Being of a leathery consistency, cockles stay on the hook well, whether ledgered or trotted, and sink quickly to the bottom. Two go nicely on a size 6, while a single cockle is best offered on a size 8 or 10 hook.

Small fish

If I had to choose one species of small fish to catch barbel, it would be the humble but readily available minnow. Small dace, gudgeon, loach, even tiny chub, will all score, but by comparison with these the minnow has a succulent softness about its silvery body. In all probability, the barbel has no such preference, merely a desire to eat for survival and will chew up just about any fishy titbit that happens its way.

Baby lampreys, which are in fact no larger than a big lobworm, are also well worth trying when you can find them. They collect in numbers in the thick bottom silt that forms behind bridge supports or in old tyres or buckets lying half-buried on the bottom in slack parts of the river. Lampreys and minnows (any small fish) are best ledgered static or rolled slowly through the swim, hooked once only through the mouth with a size 6 hook tied direct.

PARTICLES

Hempseed

Way out in front, in fact streaks ahead of all other particle attractor baits, is stewed hempseed. No other bait puts barbel into a feeding mood, sometimes even a frenzy, so effectively or as quickly as these magical seeds, which can be scattered into the head of the run by hand, catapulted accurately, or deposited on the bottom of fast, deep or distant swims with a blockend swimfeeder. For fast and deep swims fished 'under the rod tip' the hemp is best deposited with a bait-dropper.

Owing to overuse, this fabulous, magical bait is banned on some of the more popular fisheries. This is a great pity because, in complete contrast to maggots, which either carry on downstream with the flow and out of the swim or

are eagerly devoured by small fish, hempseed gets caught up among the sand and gravel on the river-bed and generally only interests larger fish. So if you distribute a pint or two of hempseed on the bottom, unless the barbel (and chub) eat it up immediately, it remains there until they find it. Attractor baits like maggots, on the other hand, have next to no holding power, especially during the warm months when nuisance species like minnows, bleak and dace are at their most active.

Preparation

To prepare hempseed, put it into a bucket with a rip-off lid and cover with boiling water. Press the lid down firmly and leave the seeds to stew in their own juices for a minimum of 24 hours, during which time they will expand and split. Surplus water can then be strained off, and the seeds will be very much darker, almost black, with tiny white shoots protruding. They are ready for immediate use.

Any surplus can be packed into polybags (a pint or two

To deposit particle baits down on to the bottom of fast or distant swims exactly where the barbel are lying, you require a comprehensive supply of swimfeeders. Remember to enlarge the holes of the feeder used for pre-baiting so that the load is emptied quickly, allowing you to retrieve the moment the feeder hits bottom.

Opposite *Hempseed and luncheon meat is the all-time best bait combination for catching barbel, wherever you fish.*

per bag) and popped into the freezer for future use. For many years now, I have prepared hempseed in bulk, a gallon or two at a time, which is much cheaper. Soaking the seeds in boiling water is far less messy than stewing them on the cooker, ruining a good saucepan and creating a terrible smell. How my mother put up with me as a fanatical teenage angler, I'll never know.

Incidentally, many other particle baits can be prepared in exactly the same way as hempseed, such as tares, tick beans, maple peas, peanuts, stewed wheat. With really hard particles like maize and tiget nuts, however, soaking in an airtight bucket is simply not enough. After soaking them for a day, remove them from the bucket and pressure cook them for 20–30 minutes. The maize grains will then split just like stewed wheat, while the tiger nuts become soft and chewable. They are, after all, a health food delicacy much loved by vegetarians.

Another way of preparing tiger nuts after a day's soaking is to put a pint or so into a shallow bowl and just cover with water. Then pop into the microwave set on high for 15 minutes. Maize is more resilient, and I have never been pleased with results when using the microwave, so stick to pressure-cooking maize.

Hempseed is usually best employed as the attractor for collecting and holding a group of barbel in a particular run, in conjunction with another bait on the hook. It works especially well when presented with other particles like corn, casters, maggots, tares, maple peas, elderberries, and even mini boilies. It is also very efficient when used in conjunction with larger offerings. A cube of luncheon meat ledgered or stret-pegged over a carpet of hempseed, for instance, is probably the all-time best barbel-catching combination.

Hempseed used as hook bait can prove extremely effective when all else fails, if somewhat fiddly to present. The best way of making a good mouthful is to string several seeds together on a fine hair with a needle, as in fig. 15A. I much prefer the softness of fly-tying thread for making the hair, which should be no longer than 1 in, otherwise the barbel is quite liable to become hooked on the outside of its mouth. Alternatively, you can use 1 lb test mono to make the hair.

Another method of presenting the stringer of seeds is

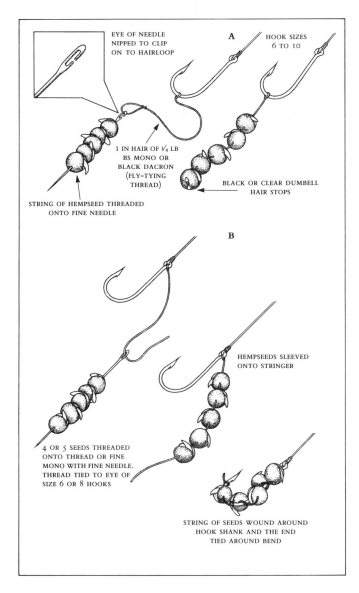

EYE OF NEEDLE
NIPPED TO CLIP
ON TO HAIRLOOP

A   HOOK SIZES
         6 TO 10

I IN HAIR OF 3/4 LB
BS MONO OR
BLACK DACRON
(FLY-TYING
THREAD)

BLACK OR CLEAR DUMBELL
HAIR STOPS

STRING OF HEMPSEED THREADED
ONTO FINE NEEDLE

B

HEMPSEEDS SLEEVED
ONTO STRINGER

4 OR 5 SEEDS THREADED
ONTO THREAD OR FINE
MONO WITH FINE NEEDLE.
THREAD TIED TO EYE OF
SIZE 6 OR 8 HOOKS

STRING OF SEEDS WOUND AROUND
HOOK SHANK AND THE END
TIED AROUND BEND

FIGURE 15 *Hair
rigged hemp stringers*

shown in fig. 15B. This time the fine thread is tied to the
eye of the hook and the seeds are sleeved on with the aid of
a thin needle. The stringer is then wound tightly around
the hook shank and down to the bend, where it is tied off.
This produces a realistic bait, but is rather tiresome as a
new hair must be tied to the eye each time when renewing
the string of seeds. To ring the changes, other small
particles like casters and tares can be mixed in with the
hempseed hair stringer.

Pre-baiting

By far the most effective way of ensuring sport from
barbel inhabiting small to medium-sized rivers is by pre-
baiting, and there is no finer routine for attracting them to
a chosen spot than by introducing stewed hempseed on a
regular basis. If you can pre-bait during the evening, say an
hour before dark, when barbel invariably start to become
active, then so much the better for they will be on to the
seeds before chub start mopping it all up. Scatter about 1 pt
(2 pt where chub are prolific), to which a handful of hook
samples has been added, into the head of the swim for
several consecutive evenings prior to fishing. There is
nothing to stop you hedging your bets by keeping two or
three swims going simultaneously, enabling a switch from
one to another as sport dictates.

*A lovely brace of
specimen barbel from
the upper reaches of
Norfolk's River
Wensum – proof of the
importance John puts
on pre-baiting.*

Tares

Although tares are not so effective as a loose-feed attractor
bait compared to hempseed, they work well and are
prepared by stewing in the same way until soft enough for
hooking. They work nicely in conjunction with hempseed,
or they can be used as both attractor and hook bait. Present
one on a size 14 hook or three up on a size 10 when the
barbel are really feeding confidently.

Tick beans

Though more commonly used as a particle bait for carp,
there is no reason why, once softened sufficiently for
hooking, this large, naturally dark-coloured bean cannot
be used confidently to catch barbel. Its size permits a single
bean to be presented on a size 10 or 8 hook, or two up on
an 8 or 6. If refused repeatedly on the hook, rig two or
three on a 1-in long hair (see fig. 16A).

Maple peas

Maples are sold as pigeon feed in corn stores and pet shops,
but once stewed this initially hard particle provides an ideal

FIGURE 16 *Particle hook-bait presentation*

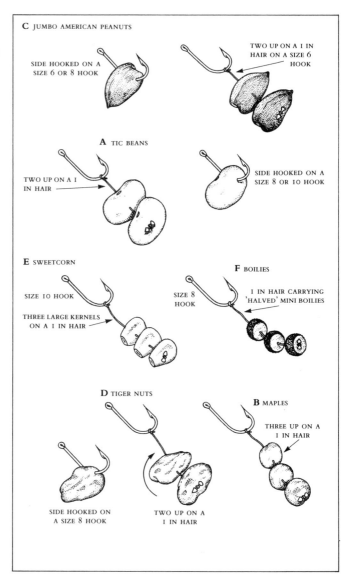

barbel bait because, like tick beans, maples are impervious to the attentions of small nuisance fish that all too quickly consume the softer alternatives such as casters, maggots and sweetcorn.

Present maples singly on a size 12, or two up on a size 8. For educated barbel, present on the hair rig (see fig. 16B). Both tick beans and maple seem to work best in conjunction with stewed hempseed as the attractor, so don't forget to add a handful to the loose feed.

Peanuts

Although it may take a while (perhaps a few days of pre-baiting) for barbel to acquire a liking for peanuts, these are a superb bait that, being firm and large, attract only barbel (and, of course, the ever ravenous chub and river carp). So the peanut is a most selective bait. I prefer the jumbo American variety that, when prepared (in the same way as hempseed), are presented one up on a size 8 or 6 hook. Standard-sized nuts fit one to a size 10 and two to a size 6. Obviously they can be hair-rigged to tempt super-cautious barbel (fig. 16C).

To accustom barbel to the taste of peanuts, crunch up a handful into small fragments and add, together with a few whole nuts, to the hempseed for pre-baiting.

Tiger nuts

Once softened (see hempseed preparation) present tiger nuts one up on a size 8 on the hook or two up on a hair (fig. 16D) and add a handful to the hempseed for attraction. As with peanuts, it may well take several sessions of fishing or pre-baiting for barbel to acquire a taste for this crunchy particle bait.

Elderberries

When long trotting the old River Lea in Hertfordshire for barbel during my early to late teens, I found that elderberries were always an excellent bait for autumn barbel. When presented in conjunction with loose-fed hempseed, the barbel could be seen easily through the clear water competing for the berries among dace, roach and chub, sometimes as far as 2 ft above the gravel bottom.

A single, ripe berry fits neatly on to a size 14 or 12 hook, but be gentle because the inside juices are all too easily squeezed out. Stretches of river that regularly produce barbel to trotted berries are those where elder trees hang out over the swim and provide food for the occupants during strong autumn winds.

I prefer to fish with ripe berries, and they can be bottled

Having sucked up an offering of quiver-tipped sweetcorn, this barbel was caught by John from a shallow run between thick weedbeds right in the middle of the day.

successfully for use at any time during the summer months by collecting a batch the previous autumn and preserving in a dilute solution of formalin or in glycerine. Use a screw-top jar. Do not strip the berries, simply cut them into small bunches and pack loosely. They will remain firm until used.

Sweetcorn

Coming close behind hempseed, caster, worms and maggots in popularity, sweetcorn is without question one of the most successful of all barbel baits. Its distinct colour, its unique sweet smell, the fact that it attracts in particle form (as opposed to just a few large offerings), are all part of its very special magic.

In stretches where corn has yet to be tried, the barbel are quite liable to respond quickly and aggressively, sometimes within hours of its initial introduction, especially after a few pre-baiting stints. In clear rivers where corn has been used exhaustively over many years, however, it is interesting to observe how barbel react to its sudden arrival in the swim. Some fish will totally ignore its existence while others (with long memories) will panic and vacate the swim the very second they set eyes upon that yellow carpet on the river-bed.

By the same token, it is also fair to say that many anglers forget entirely about sweetcorn once it has blown, and after a period of non-use it tends to take on a new lease of life, although it is seldom anywhere near as devastating as when it is offered to barbel for the very first time. This, incidentally, is true of many of the different kinds of bait with the exception, perhaps, of hempseed.

To extend the catching life of corn, it can be coloured using a little hot water mixed into a dish with a spoonful of powder carp-bait dye. Red and brown are colours worth trying.

As with all particles, present it off the hook on a fine, 1 in hair if bites are not forthcoming with a basic presentation (see fig. 16E).

Stewed wheat

This inexpensive grain is economical when you are pre-baiting numerous swims. Once stewed so that the skin cracks to reveal the soft white inner, it has a distinct nutty aroma and is a fine bait, both as hook bait and loose feed. Alternatively, add a handful to the hempseed for attracting barbel into the swim and into a feeding mood, and use wheat on the hook. Two grains on a size 10 or 3 to size 8 provide a good mouthful for barbel. Like corn, wheat can also be dyed, so there is much room for experimentation with different colours.

Maize

Tougher than wheat, even when prepared (see hempseed preparation), maize is nearly as brightly coloured as sweetcorn. Being larger, it is an ideal choice wherever shoals of nuisance fish, such as dace or small roach, incessantly peck at sweetcorn on the hook. A much underrated and rarely used bait for barbel, it is well worth the extra effort in preparation.

Boilies

Though boilies are associated in the main with carp and tench fishing, barbel also love them once a taste has been acquired, and while boilies are not generally considered a 'particle', by mixing a handful of mini-boilies with hempseed for loose-feed attraction, they can be treated as one. On the hook try a larger boilie, either side-hooked or on a hair, or a string of, say, three mini-boilies of the kind added to the loose feed. I am inclined to suggest you opt for darker colours rather than bright, but then yellow mini-boilies are extremely effective and provide a natural follow-on from sweetcorn once its pulling power starts to wane. As for flavours, any savoury, cheese or shellfish flavour is worth trying.

So that barbel quickly acquire a taste for boilies, cut minis in half and mix them with the hempseed attractor. If bites do not happen with whole boilies side-hooked (two on a size 8), try a hair string of halves (see fig. 16F).

The best aspect of boilies is that, like other hard particles, they are impervious to the attentions of smaller, nuisance species, although it goes without saying that chub will soon be on to them.

MEAT

Tinned meat

While many a barbel enthusiast swears by and will use only a particular brand of luncheon meat, chopped pork roll or ham, for the purpose of simplicity and not wishing to turn this chapter into a shopping guide, I shall treat all tinned

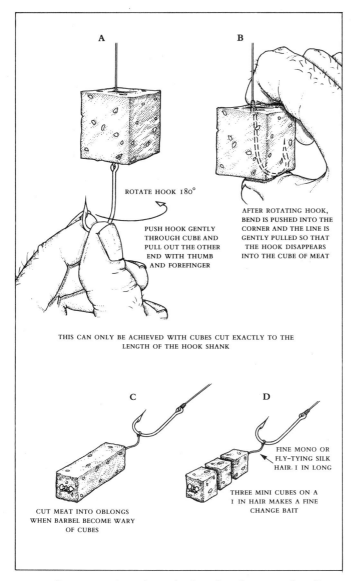

FIGURE 17 *Presenting cubed meat*

A

B

ROTATE HOOK 180°

PUSH HOOK GENTLY
THROUGH CUBE AND
PULL OUT THE OTHER
END WITH THUMB
AND FOREFINGER

AFTER ROTATING HOOK,
BEND IS PUSHED INTO THE
CORNER AND THE LINE IS
GENTLY PULLED SO THAT
THE HOOK DISAPPEARS
INTO THE CUBE OF MEAT

THIS CAN ONLY BE ACHIEVED WITH CUBES CUT EXACTLY TO THE
LENGTH OF THE HOOK SHANK

C

D

FINE MONO OR
FLY-TYING SILK
HAIR. 1 IN LONG

CUT MEAT INTO OBLONGS
WHEN BARBEL BECOME WARY
OF CUBES

THREE MINI CUBES ON A
1 IN HAIR MAKES A FINE
CHANGE BAIT

meats firm enough to be cubed under the same heading. And that includes just about everything with the exception of corned beef, which is too crumbly.

However, there are very noticeable and important differences between one brand and another, and between one type of tinned meat and another. Some are fattier than others, which makes them more buoyant (useful when fishing over thick bottom weed). Others are more dense and so stay on the hook better and keep on the bottom in fast currents, reasonably impervious to the attentions of

Whether cut into squares or oblongs and put straight onto the hook, or presented on a fine hair rig, tinned meats offer enormous scope to the barbel enthusiast, so shop around.

tiny shoal fish, which seem to be forever nibbling away. So experiment by trying different brands.

The secret of fishing using meat is to be happy about presentation and confident that your cube will not fly off the hook during casting, so learn to cut the meat into equal-sized cubes (using a fine, long-bladed knife) no longer than the shank of the hook being used (see fig. 17A). It is then a simple matter of pushing the hook through the cube and easing it out the other side without splitting the meat. Ease the bend of the hook into one of the corners and gently pull on the line (fig. 17B). The hook becomes hidden from view and easy to cast. And as the meat is soft, the hook will easily pull through the bait and into the barbel on the strike.

When barbel repeatedly refuse meat on the hook, present it on a 1-in long, fine hair, which gives them greater confidence (fig. 17C). The shape can be changed to an oblong when the cube becomes familiar to the barbel and they can be seen to react against it. Alternatively, cut the meat into mini cubes and present three or four on a hair (fig. 17D).

Meat in skins

As an exploratory trip to the chilled meat counter at the local supermarket or delicatessen will immediately prove, there is a wonderful, almost endless, choice of sausage-type (skinned) meats, and barbel love them all. In a narrow format there are chippolata sausages, spicey sausages, tinned sausages both large and small, and even small cocktail sausages, all of which may be cut into ½-in sections and securely hooked through the tough skin. For loose feed, either scatter a handful of sections cut to the same size into the head of the swim every so often, or, if you are loose feeding with stewed hempseed as the main attractor, dice the sausage up into tiny cubes and mix it in thoroughly.

The larger sausage types, up to 3 in in diameter, such as garlic-based German sausage, smoked sausage, black pudding and so on, are best presented as you would luncheon meat and other tinned meats, by removing the outer skin and cutting into cubes or oblongs of the desired sizes with a thin, long-bladed knife.

Any type of spicy sausage in a skin is potentially a fine barbel bait. They keep well, are firm in consistency for hooking, and you can always eat them yourself if the barbel are not interested.

PASTES

Sausage-meat

Plain sausage-meat, either beef or pork, purchased by the pound from the local butcher, makes a fine bait for barbel. It is far too sticky to be used on its own, but you can make it into a firm paste by kneading cornflour into it, and this can be used for both hook baits and loose feed. Sausage-meat paste can be popped into the freezer for future use.

Trout pellet paste

One of the most effective pastes for catching barbel that have seen and been taken on all the popular baits can be made quite easily from trout pellets, or any similar pelleted pond-fish food.

To make a large ball of paste (any surplus can be frozen for future use), put 2 pt of pellets into a bowl and liberally soak with hot water. Leave for half an hour for the water to be absorbed, and then knead into a firm paste adding cornflour if required to blot up any excess water. Use a thumbnail-sized knob to cover a size 6 hook and scatter in loose fragments at regular intervals to attract fish.

Cheese

Another great paste for barbel can be made by mixing together equal parts of grated cheddar cheese and mashed bread. Start by soaking several slices of stale bread in cold water, and after squeezing out the excess, knead until you have a creamy paste. At this point, add the grated cheese and continue kneading until it has an even, fairly stiff consistency. Any type of hard cheese can be used, although plain cheddar is best.

It is well worth taking time to evaluate the huge variety of cheese available at the local supermarket. Some brands of processed cheese, for instance, can be kneaded and used as a paste without any additions, or cut into cubes with a fine, long-bladed knife and presented on a short hair rig, in exactly the same way as cubed meat.

Wherever nuisance species are prolific, the best way to

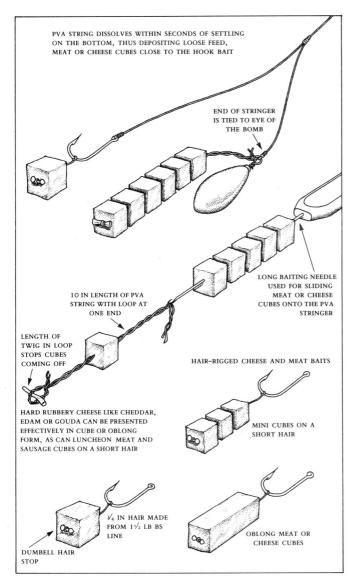

FIGURE 18 *PVA
stringer rig, and hair-
rigged cube baits*

deter them is to use rubbery cheese such as gouda or edam,
either cubed or cut into oblongs.

If you want to deposit loose-feed cheese or meat cubes
on the bottom of fast, deep-water swims, you cannot do so
accurately enough by throwing them in well upstream. In
fact, this could well encourage barbel to follow them
downstream and out of the swim if your estimation of
current strength is a little out. The quickest way to get
them into the swim is to rig up a 6 in stringer of PVA with

John's brother, Dave
Wilson, brings a
barbel gently upstream
against the pressure of
fast, shallow water on
the River Lea. The
bait was a lump of
freelined cheese paste.

a loop at one end. Slide on a batch of cubes with the aid of a long baiting needle (see fig. 18). The end of the stringer is then tied to the eye of the ledger bomb. Once the bomb settles, you can be certain (when the PVA dissolves) that the loose-feed cubes will lie close to the hook bait.

Bread

Last and by no means least (my largest-ever barbel of 12¾ lb was caught on bread flake), we come to plain white bread.

I have already mentioned mashed bread in the making of cheese paste, but bread can be used in another way to make a wonderful groundbait for ledgering or trotting with either bread flake or bread crust on the hook. Soak an old

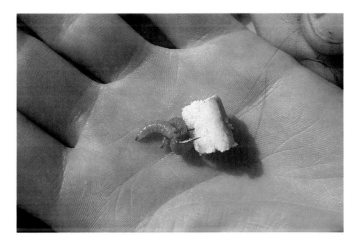

Using its inherent buoyancy for easing the bait over bottom debris, a cube of crust is balanced with three lively maggots. What sensible barbel can refuse such a feast?

loaf or some bread scraps for a couple of hours, and after squeezing out all the excess water pulp it between your fingers into a mash. When feeding the swim, squeeze it again into golf-ball sized pieces and throw well upstream so that they break up and keep a steady trickle of particles trundling along the bottom.

A large lump of breadflake taken from the inside of a fresh white loaf and pressed hard along the hook shank will stay on surprisingly well, regardless of current strength. Use a thumbnail-sized piece on a size 10 hook or a golf-ball-sized lump on a size 6.

Bread attracts barbel all season, and is especially effective during the milder spells in winter. Then I like to offer breadcrust if stret-pegging or long trotting. A ¼-in or ⅜-in cube of tough crust (from the bottom of a tin loaf) on a size 10 hook makes a fine bait. Do not forget to pinch on a dust shot a few inches away so that the bait is presented close to the bottom, not way above the barbel's head.

CHAPTER SIX

TECHNIQUES AND RIGS

FREELINING

The very first introduction of barbel into the River Wensum originated from an exchange deal in the early 1960s, consisting of 35 Norfolk bream in the 4–6 lb range swapped for 30 barbel of similar stamp from the Yorkshire Ouse. This was arranged through the respective river boards, as was a second stocking in 1971 with barbel from the River Severn. This leads me to the very first barbel I caught from the River Wensum, which came from a narrow, shallow stretch one early October morning. It was about a year after the stocking, and I was enjoying a meandering session freelining lobs and slugs for chub.

With the sun barely above the horizon, visibility through the clear water was rather poor. Nevertheless, behind a thick weedbed in the middle of the river I could just make out the rear end of a very long fish that was obviously not a pike. I slipped a couple of large lobs on to the size 4 hook and flipped them well upstream and behind the weedbed, hoping the flow would allow them to settle on the bottom a little in front of the mystery fish – which I half-expected to be a large brown trout.

The line slowly eased downstream in a nice bow for several feet as the worms tumbled along, then it twitched slightly before tightening positively. I struck hard immediately and was flabbergasted to see the unmistakeable shape of a barbel hit the surface in a huge swirl before it dived and motored upstream towards a line of alders fringing the opposite bank. I managed to steer it clear of the sunken branches and after a short, spirited fight, I bustled it eagerly into the landing net. At a shade over 7 lb it was no monster, but was to my knowledge one of the first barbel to come from the Wensum. The event also proved the effectiveness of freelining for barbel in certain circumstances and particularly in very clear rivers that are not too fast. There is little point, for instance, in lobbing in a feeder right on top of a fish that has been visually pinpointed at close range in slow-moving water. It does not need attracting, it is already there. Baits like a lobworm (use two on the hook to aid casting), a lump of cheese paste, a meat cube, etc, are absolutely ideal and have enough inherent weight to be cast easily and accurately over distances of 20 to 30 ft with a simple underarm swing, even with the hook tied direct to 6 lb test.

Even particles such as several grains of sweetcorn packed on to a size 6 hook can be freelined through the swim with the help of a swan shot or two pinched on the line 1 ft or so above the hook. If you find that any more weight is required to hold the bait steady, you move on to straight ledgering.

I particularly enjoy freelining shallow swims close into the bank where barbel rest beneath weed rafts and the like or behind boulders. Sometimes they grab for the bait as the current tumbles it along on a completely free (shotless) line. Sometimes they seem loathe to intercept, and will only suck the bait up once it settles static on the bottom.

When casting upstream beside rafts of weed or behind clumps of bullrushes and watching the line for bites, slowly recover the slack as the bait is brought downstream by the current. Watch that line like a hawk where it enters the water, and remember to keep the rod-tip high. Some bites cause the line to fall slack suddenly (drop backs) as a barbel inhales the bait and turns immediately downstream. If the barbel moves across the current or carries on swimming upstream, the bow will steadily tighten after a preliminary twitch or two. Either way, you will be in no doubt that a barbel has taken your freelined offering so strike at once.

Freelining is a fascinating and extremely mobile technique that allows you freedom to roam from swim to swim and really search the bottom of all likely runs by continually casting to a different spot if you cannot see the barbel, and work the bait down naturally. Alternatively, you can cast to individual fish and on occasions watch

Camouflaged within a thick marginal hedge of nettles and willow-herb stems, John trundles a lobworm through a shallow run in his local River Wensum. Close-range freelining is one of the most exciting ways of tempting summer barbel when the water is both warm and clear and their exact position can be pinpointed.

them extend their protrusible mouths and hoover up the bait.

QUIVERTIP LEDGERING

Because the current speed in the majority of favourite barbel runs makes it necessary to anchor the bait to the bottom (or rolled gently across), and because many such swims are also beyond casting range of presenting a freelined bait and watching the bow in the line for bites, quivertip ledgering combines the most sensitive technique and method of bite indication yet invented.

While a fair proportion of bites will inevitably be those characteristic 'slamming takes' when quite suddenly the rod-tip is wrenched over (the barbel sets the hook itself) situations will also arise, and particularly on hard-fished and slow-moving rivers, where the softness of the quivertip allows finickety, educated barbel to hold on to the bait just that little bit longer, whether using a light, two-swan shot link or a heavy 2 oz feeder. And this allows you to capitalize on all those gentle knocks and drop-backs that only show up on a finely tapered quivertip.

The secret lies in interpreting each and every movement of the tip in relation to what is happening on the bottom, whether the indications are from small fish messing about with the bait, line bites from the barbel's pectoral or pelvic fins, or hittable knocks. For instance, a phenomenon that all barbel fishermen experience is a sandpapery feeling on the line (when hooked around the ball of the index finger) or gentle vibration on the quivertip immediately before it is wrenched over. As I mentioned in Chapter 2, what actually happens is that in centralizing its underslung mouth in an aggressive side-to-side movement over your bait, the barbel's long whiskers rub against the line. It then turns around or moves across the bottom or even upstream, immediately feeling the build up of pressure on the line (just like bolt-rig fishing for carp), closes its mouth and does a runner. At this point the hook is usually driven home by the fish's own weight, and if you are not careful the rod itself might even be pulled in seconds afterwards. I know far more anglers who have experienced the humiliation of having their rod pulled in when barbel fishing than when fishing for carp. So remember never to look or turn round while leaving your rod unattended on the rod-rest. When they go, rods fly into the river with surprising speed and disappear in seconds. In fact, only when bites are really

Having catapulted a carpet of hempseed into a deep run along the opposite bank of Worcestershire's lovely little River Teme (a tributary of the Severn), Eddie Foster from Leicester waits for a barbel to accept his bunch of quivertipped casters.

few and far between do I not actually hold the rod. And even then, it is supported on a pair of rests close to hand, with the tip angled upwards in fast swims to alleviate undue current pressure against the line.

When I expect fish to bite regularly, I use a front rod-rest only, with the last 12–16 in of the rod butt resting across my right knee. My striking hand then rests relaxed yet ready on top of the handle, fingers loosely held around the reel stem in readiness for an instant strike.

When anticipating action, I always hook the index finger (at the first joint) of my right hand around the line. My mind and eyes can then even wander around, enjoying the natural history, because the slightest pull or relaxation of the line is instantly transmitted to the soft, super-sensitive finger pad. Touch is a sense we do not use enough when fishing, relying perhaps more than we should on sight alone. Shut your eyes and gently pull a length of monofilament line across the pad of your index finger and you will appreciate why touch ledgering in conjunction with a quivertip is so effective. With aggressive species like barbel (and chub), some kind of registration is nearly always felt on the pad of the index finger immediately prior to the tip going over or springing back.

Drop-backs

In most swims it is best to cast downstream and allow the rig to swing across to the head of the run, using just enough weight to hold bottom. Bites are then invariably good pull-rounds as the barbel turns downstream or moves across the current. However, even when fishing directly downstream you do experience the odd occasion when the tip suddenly springs back and you sit there perplexed waiting for something to happen. If you look carefully, you can watch the line slowly following the route of the unsuspecting barbel as it moves upstream completely oblivious or unconcerned about towing the ledger rig.

More drop-backs will occur when casting across the flow to distant swims in big rivers such as the Thames or Severn, and a word about rod position is in order because the further out that you fish directly across the flow, the

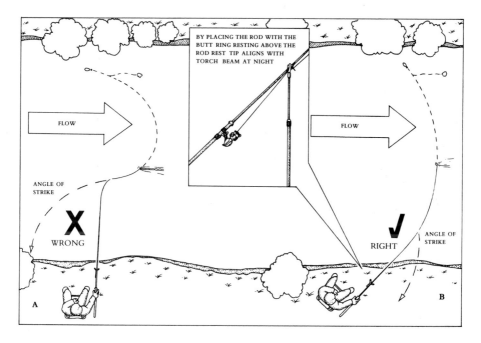

BY PLACING THE ROD WITH THE BUTT RING RESTING ABOVE THE ROD REST TIP ALIGNS WITH TORCH BEAM AT NIGHT

FLOW

FLOW

ANGLE OF STRIKE

X

WRONG

✓

RIGHT

ANGLE OF STRIKE

A

B

greater is the bow in the line (created by current pressure) between bait and quivertip. Consider fig. 19A where an enormous bow forms if the rod is positioned straight out but not high enough, which results in more line being affected by current pressure. Extra weight is then required to hold bottom, in addition to bites being missed through an inefficient striking curve. The position shown in fig. 19B makes far more sense.

Incidentally, when casting to swims beyond the accurate range of the catapult, the best way to introduce loose feed to attract barbel is with the aid of a large blockend swimfeeder. Five or ten minutes spent casting and recasting to lay a thick carpet of hempseed (including a few hook-bait samples) on the bottom of the swim at the start of a session is time well spent. Do not forget to enlarge the holes of the (pre-baiting) feeder with a pair of scissors so that its load washes out within a second or two of it hitting bottom. And do not worry about the splash it makes as it goes in. On most well-fished barbel rivers, the occupants of the swim might even be rooting about among the seeds before you have finished the pre-baiting. Then again, well-educated barbel may make you wait an hour or so before they move up into the swim and over the seeds. If bites do not materialize within a few minutes, do not be tempted

FIGURE 19 *Quivertip ledgering across the flow in larger rivers*

After slowly working his way in chest-waders through extensive beds of potomogeton and rununculus to fish for barbel in a narrow run beneath a large willow on the Hampshire Avon at Christchurch, John lands a modest fish on quivertipped sweetcorn.

into throwing in another helping of loose feed (see Pre-baiting, page 79). Be patient, the whiskers will come.

Casting upstream

On most rivers there will always be a percentage of swims that can only be tackled successfully by casting directly upstream against the flow, using just enough weight to hold bottom so that the barbel feel minimal resistance when moving off with the bait. Bites are sudden, dramatic drop-backs, the quivertip flipping backwards as the line falls completely slack.

Generally, a long, sweeping strike will drive the hook home, but odd occasions arise when you need to wind like mad in order to recover most of the line as the barbel swims several yards towards you before you can make a successful strike.

Swims with excellent potential are ignored by many anglers because they cannot cast the bait downstream and across in the accepted manner, and loose feed thrown in

Following two exceptionally spirited scraps within the confines of a small, snaggy swim on Norfolk's River Wensum, John carefully returns a brace of large barbel. Both gave classic drop-back bites to ledgered luncheon meat cubes cast upstream to the edge of a weedraft.

With the water still holding colour following heavy rain, John prepares to net a River Teme barbel that succumbed to a caster and swim-feedered hemp combination, ledgered upstream along the opposite bank beside overhanging willows.

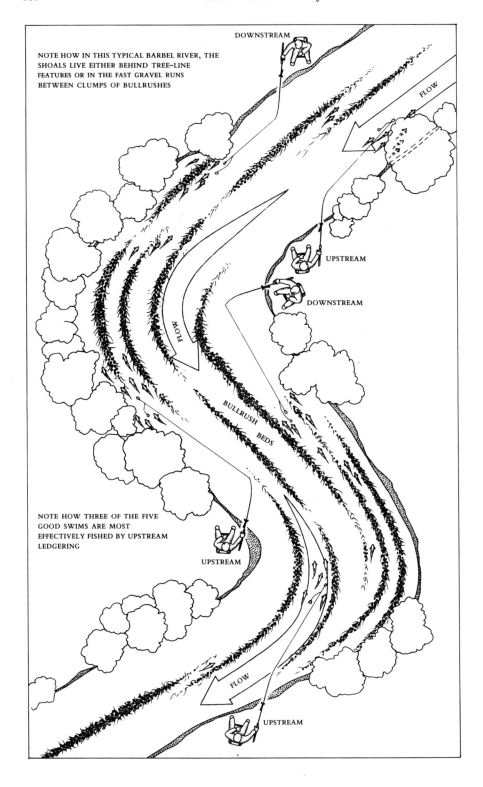

is taken down by the current. Fig. 20 illustrates an example
of a river in which barbel occupy runs behind the tree-line
features and in runs between bullrush beds. However,
three of the five swims can be fished effectively only by
ledgering upstream. Moreover, loose feeding with either a
particle attractor such as hempseed or fragments of the
hook bait, or both, is not as difficult as it may first seem. In
most instances, the problem is solved by quietly walking
upstream, parallel with the head of the swim, and
catapulting the bait out a little upstream of the shoal.

FIGURE 20 *Upstream ledgering*

If overhanging trees or tall beds of dense bullrushes
prevent you catapulting in loose feed upstream, use a
blockend feeder for depositing baits like hemp, casters or
maggots; or make up a PVA (plastic vinyl acetate)
dissolving stringer and tie it to the bomb swivel, as in fig.
18, p. 89, when presenting large offerings such as meat
cubes or cheese paste.

When to step down

There is no doubt that just as other popular species become
conditioned by regular attention and over-fishing, barbel
also learn the ropes, becoming extremely choosey and
cautious.

I remember a time on Worcestershire's lovely little River
Teme at Lyndridge, a location selected for one of my *Go
Fishing* television programmes, where I had certainly not
bargained for the barbel being so well educated. The
particular stretch I had chosen was heavily match-fished at
weekends by Birmingham AA members, and consequently
those barbel knew all about small hooks, fine lines and
blockend feeders suddenly arriving on the bottom of the
river, complete with a carpet of hempseed.

As much of my barbel fishing in recent years prior to
this was centred around stalking specimens in the Upper
Wensum, where sensible line strengths and hooks could
still be employed without scaring the fish, those Teme
barbel proved to be a real education. It seemed ridiculous
that bites did not materialize unless I stepped down to size
16 and 18 hooks holding a single or double caster to a 2 lb
bottom, but this was the case. No doubt, eventually one
would have plucked up enough courage to take a lump of

Holding his Avon quivertip rod in a relaxed yet expectant mood, John awaits events, having placed his ledgered sausage paste well upstream into the main flush of a large weir-pool.

sausage paste or a big lobworm on a size 6 hook tied direct to 5 lb test – there is always one – but the message came over loud and clear. When in Rome!

Obviously, to step down further, to a 20 hook and a 1 lb bottom for example, would have had those barbel really buzzing. However, as I mentioned earlier, there is a point beyond which a sensible barbel fisherman should not go. The bottom line is: do I stand more than a fair chance of landing a reasonable barbel on the tackle I am using? And ensure that your answer is always 'yes', or one day you will regret it. Besides, there is more than one way of skinning a cat, or outwitting spooky barbel. I have already described how to rig up a bait on the 'hair' (see page 89), and this simple, confidence-giving rig makes a fool of fish that have been spooked by the most popular, repeatedly used baits presented directly on the hook – baits that are offered to them week in and week out, and to which they have succumbed once too often.

Night fishing

Readiness, with eyes on the quivertip, yet relaxed, is the hallmark of an experienced barbel fisherman. And should bites not materialize, then a step down to a lighter hook length and smaller bait on a small hook is called for.

If, when stepping down in tackle or presenting the bait on a hair rig, neither appeals or produces results, you should plan to catch your barbel at the best time of all, when they are least cautious and thus at their most vulnerable – during dusk and after dark. This is the greatest leveller of all, when bites are even more suicidal than from uneducated barbel during daylight. And they nearly pull the rod in, so try not to let your eyes wander away from the rod. Even baits that are old hat suddenly start producing. Lines that educated barbel would flee from in panic on sight in clear water at midday are accepted without question. And the size of your hook will have not the slightest bearing on the number of bites received.

With baits, however, there are certain provisos. For instance, during the summer and autumn, be careful not to let smelly or animal baits such as cheese paste, a bunch of maggots, worms or even luncheon meat, linger too long on the river-bed during the hours of darkness where eels are common. And let's face it, eels are a night-time menace in most river systems.

Go for breadcrust or bread flake, sweetcorn, peanuts, etc. (see Chapter 5). As for bite indication, when ledgering

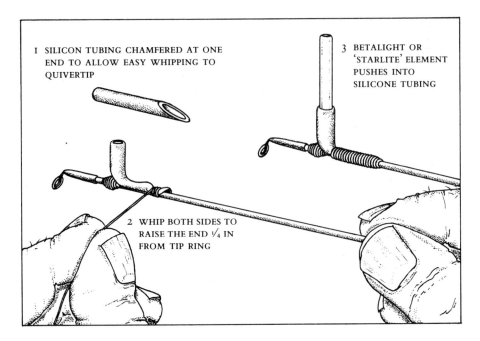

1 SILICON TUBING CHAMFERED AT ONE END TO ALLOW EASY WHIPPING TO QUIVERTIP

3 BETALIGHT OR 'STARLITE' ELEMENT PUSHES INTO SILICONE TUBING

2 WHIP BOTH SIDES TO RAISE THE END ¼ IN FROM TIP RING

FIGURE 21 *Quiver-tipping at night*

into darkness I illuminate the quivertip with a narrow-beam torch set on the ground downstream of the rod, pointing upwards and out, so it shines only on the tip and not into my eyes or on the water. This is most important, because barbel in clear water might easily become scared.

All my quivertip rods are painted matt white (two coats) along the last 16–20 in to catch every bit of light. This makes them easy to watch, even for hours at a time, and also improves daytime concentration on the quivertip in poor light conditions and against a broken background. If the rod is firmly set on two telescopic rests with the butt-ring hung up against the curve in the front rest, before the torch is positioned, the quivertip will then settle right in the middle of the torch beam every cast without further ado. As I keep a second, small torch in my jacket pocket, there is no need to move the one carefully positioned on the ground.

A second, and I think less effective, method of visual indication at night is provided by whipping a ¾-in section of silicone tubing on to the very end of the quivertip and pushing in a powerful betalight element (600 micro-lamberts), or a mini starlight chemical element, which is considerably brighter but lasts for only 6–8 hours. When fish are biting regularly, a luminous element on the end of the quivertip is quite sufficient. However, considering that there will inevitably be long periods of inactivity, coupled to occasions when bits of weed and other debris continually hit the line and register false bites, I find the torch-illuminated tip far easier to concentrate on.

ROD-TOP LEDGERING

The previous section has covered the interpretation of bites and the most effective methods to use when quivertip ledgering, and virtually the same can be said of straight rod-top ledgering. Bites register in exactly the same way, of course, but owing to the thicker, less sensitive tip most will not be seen or struck so early.

However, there are occasions when straight rod-tip ledgering is a better proposition, especially when presenting the bait in extremely fast or deep swirling water, forcing the most powerful of quivertips to bend fully round. Again, whenever the river is in full spate and carrying mountains of debris, clumps of blanket weed, large leaves and the like, it is futile to watch a super-sensitive quivertip – far better to be rod-tip ledgering.

Hitting into really hefty fish in fast, heavy currents on line strengths over 6 lb test, when it is imperative to stop the barbel from getting into snags as quickly as possible, is another occasion when I opt for a standard heavy Avon rod without a quivertip. And for bumping small deadbaits slowly across the current along deep runs, beside snaggy bankside swims, or down on the bottom of turbulent weir pools, the standard rod-tip is again the better option. Besides, the ferocity with which barbel hit and subsequently belt off with a freshly killed minnow certainly leaves you in little doubt about the bite. When the rod is almost wrenched from your grasp, a sensitive quivertip is hardly necessary. So don't be tempted to put the rod down too often when working small fish baits, although the static deadbait will still catch. Keep the bait slowly on the move by lifting the rod-tip every 30 seconds to ease the ledger weight (use just enough to hold bottom) across and down each likely-looking run – beneath weed rafts, close

Hooked on a standard Avon ledger rod only a few yards below the well-known Pipe Swim on the Royalty Fishery in Hampshire, a barbel races downstream. The fisherman could have great difficulty in bringing it back again due to the extensive weedbeds.

alongside undercut banking, below the white water in weir-pools, etc.

If you wish, this can be an impatient, mobile, exploring method. You need not rely on attracting a shoal of barbel into a certain spot in order to take several fish. You simply wander upstream or down, probing with the deadbait and spending the minimal amount of time in each swim, expecting to instigate an immediate response every so often. It is great fun because along the way anything and everything unexpected can and does grab hold in addition to the occasional barbel. The ever-hungry chub, pike, eels and perch, and in game rivers, trout especially.

Bear in mind that you need to use fresh bait. Collect a supply of live minnows the day before or on the very morning you fish, and kill them as you use them, flicking one on the head with your forefinger immediately before hooking it on (see page 73).

FLOATFISHING

Stret pegging

The beauty of stret pegging is that it combines the benefits of both ledgering and floatfishing: optimum sensitivity with a float to watch, and a static bait anchored to the bottom exactly where you want it.

For obvious reasons, this technique can only be used for presenting the bait immediately downstream in close-range swims no more than a few feet out from the near bank. It is tailor-made for all deep, marginal runs almost regardless of current speed. Those swims where the bottom consists of clean sand or gravel, and where marginal sedges, reeds or rushes hang out over the water forming a cavernous raft overhead, are adored by barbel and can be

No wonder Wilson is smiling. A short stret-pegging session after dark in a 5-ft deep marginal swim along his local River Wensum produced this wonderful brace: a barbel of 12¼ lb and a roach weighing 2 lb 7 oz. Both accepted bread flake on a size 8 hook tied direct to 6 lb test, as did also a 4 lb 6 oz chub and a 10½ lb mirror carp taken during the same session.

more effectively fished by stret-pegging than ledgering.

The value of this seemingly insensitive technique can be appreciated by studying fig. 22. A biting fish feels no immediate resistance, as it would with a ledgered bait where the line is taut between ledger weight and rod-tip. It may suck the bait up freely and move off before the bow starts to straighten and the float submerges in a glorious, confident bite. It is imperative that the float is fixed at both ends with silicone rubber-bands and set at more than twice the depth to encourage an accentuated bow to form in the line between the float and the bottom shots. And here lies the secret. As long as the bow that is pushed downstream by the flow is large enough, only the middle section creates resistance against the current pressure. This permits the float to lie perfectly flat (and not drag under), swaying gently from side to side on the surface until the bait is taken.

My favourite float for this is an unpainted, 8 in length of thickish peacock quill. For extremely fast, broken water a large chubber or an Avon-style float with a thickish body will ride better. However, it must lie flat on the surface once the bait and shots are in position, or the technique cannot work effectively. So if you are tackling really fast swims, be prepared to keep pushing the float further up the line until it does lie flat once the end rig has settled.

Now for the end rig. To fish slow currents, simply pinch on a swan shot 10 in above the hook. In slightly faster runs, opt for two swan shots. For stronger currents, retain the single swan shot 10 in above the hook and transfer any additional weights required, such as swan shots, a bomb or a small blockend feeder, to a mini ledger link constructed from a small ring and 1–2 in of 10 lb mono (fig. 22).

If you work at keeping very still and quiet and sit well back from the edge, it is surprising, even in crystal-clear water, how ridiculously close in you can encourage barbel to feed by stret pegging. The cast should be an easy underarm flick made downstream and slightly across, so that the rig swings inwards and immediately below the float (see fig. 22). Sit facing downstream with the rod angled slightly upwards on two rests to keep all the line from float to rod tip off the surface. A 12 ft, 1¼ lb test curve, carbon Avon with 6 lb line is perfect for the job.

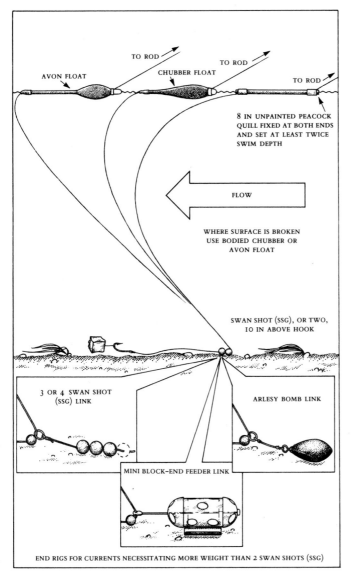

FIGURE 22 *Stret pegging*

Fragments of loose feed or particle attractors such as hempseed can be deposited accurately by hand a few yards upstream, where current speed is minimal. For fast runs, use a bait-dropper to lay a carpet of hempseed or sweetcorn or employ a small blockend feeder as an integral part of the rig. The feeder set-up is particularly useful when fishing for winter barbel, which are usually loathe to move far in cold water conditions. At such times the hook bait must lie close to the loose attractor feed.

*Ray Page of
Cheshunt fishes for
barbel in the bubbly
water of an overshoot
weir-pool on the
River Lea's Relief
Channel with stret-
pegging float tackle.*

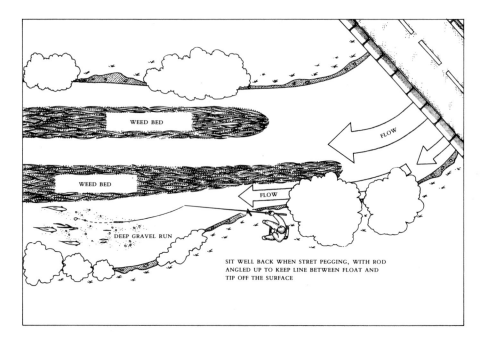

WEED BED

FLOW

WEED BED

FLOW

DEEP GRAVEL RUN

SIT WELL BACK WHEN STRET PEGGING, WITH ROD
ANGLED UP TO KEEP LINE BETWEEN FLOAT AND
TIP OFF THE SURFACE

FIGURE 23 *Stret pegging*

Once you catch barbel by stret pegging, you will want to seek out swims specifically to enjoy the method, and practised after dark it is both fascinating and deadly. There are two ways to make the stem of peacock quill (or a thick waggler) luminous. Either glue into the tip a 600 micro-lambert power, luminous betalight element (after removing the centre pith to the depth of 3/16 in with a pin and whipping over to strengthen it), which I find quite easy to watch at close range; or add a standard-size starlight or Drennan chemical luminous element, with a ½ in length of silicone float tubing. These elements last for several hours and are exceptionally bright once you bend the casing and shake, which mixes and activates the chemicals inside.

Stret pegging is one of those methods that works at all times throughout the season, because it allows you to place the bait extremely accurately, whether barbel are holed up in a narrow run between beds of summer marginal weed or hugging the inside of an acute bend during a rip-roaring winter's flood.

Long trotting

In classic barbel rivers, which are quite shallow and thus easy to wade and where shoals hug the clean gravel and sandy runs between beds of long, flowing streamer weeds, it is an absolute joy to catch barbel by long trotting. Indeed, many such areas contain good concentrations of fish throughout the summer months, in runs so narrow the occupants could never be offered a bait let alone be caught from the bankside using ledgering techniques. You get the best results by climbing quietly into the river in thigh boots or chest-waders (a sound investment), and wading slowly to an upstream position, from which the bait can be trotted almost directly downstream. This permits excellent presentation because the float is not dragged off course when it is controlled or held back. The bait can be trundled down in a natural way along the desired line by gently breaking the float's passage and occasionally swinging it upwards by holding the float back hard momentarily.

Long trotting will, of course, also produce barbel from just about any weed-free run where the river-bed is reasonably consistent in depth. In rivers that run on the coloured side, there is obviously some work to be done with the plummet. The key is to study surface patterns and choose swims that are fast but steady, where the barbel are not forced to change direction every few seconds. Look especially for filter lines, strips of water between turbulence and the smooth, slower currents. These contain the largest shoals of all, numbers of fish hugging the bottom in wait for the natural food that the main flush keeps sending across their field of vision.

As the barbel feeds from the bottom and the layer of water immediately above the river-bed where food particles are washed along by the current, your bait needs to be presented either dragging bottom (only possible where the river-bed consists of clean sand or gravel) or within a few inches of the bottom. Any higher and it will ride above the barbel's head, out of its feeding zone. In the summer months when the water runs both warm and crystal clear, barbel will take, and can sometimes be observed, moving upwards and across the flow to intercept loose-fed casters and maggots as they fall and tumble downriver. Such occasions are responsible for those unmistakeable bites that drag the float quickly beneath the surface within a second or so of your holding it back to waver the bait upwards. Generally speaking, however, barbel want their dinner to move slowly along or just above the river-bed.

Long trotting is a mobile, searching, probing method of locating barbel. When wading in shallow, clear water, John gently shuffles his feet around to disturb the bottom sediment. This clouds the water and releases minute food particles, which soon has the barbel in a feeding mood.

Opposite A wonderful way to catch barbel is to wade carefully out into a shallow river so that the float can be trotted directly downstream to a shoal, as Ray Page proves. The bait pouch alleviates the necessity for continually opening and closing bait tins.

Ideal baits for trotting (see Chapter 5) are the big four, maggots, casters, worms and bread, with sweetcorn bringing up the rear. As for ledgering, I rate hempseed highly for loose-feed attraction and often put a couple of handfuls into the top of each swim when long trotting, prior to following through with a bunch of maggots or casters, plus loose-feed helpings of the same every other cast. It's only fair to state that at no time when trotting for barbel should you expect to enjoy a bite every other trot down, as you might when roach fishing. The hard fact is that long trotting can prove tiring work, particularly in low water temperatures when the barbel are not really responding to a moving bait. You could well put the float beautifully through the swim ten, twenty or even thirty times before, quite suddenly, under it goes, and having struck subconsciously you are playing a barbel. On another occasion, the float may disappear on the first or second trot through – without a repeat performance, regardless of how many times the float is subsequently run through.

It goes without saying that when wading, an indispensable item of tackle is the bait pouch or apron, and so too is a tackle waistcoat. There is nothing more infuriating than having to make frequent trips back to the bank in order to

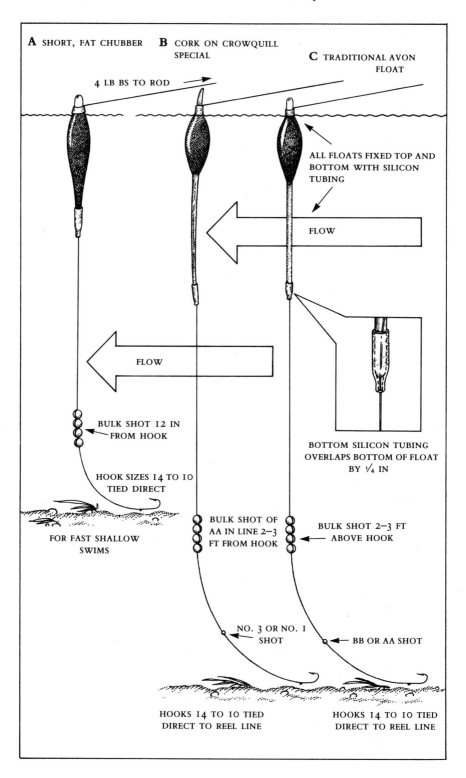

A SHORT, FAT CHUBBER   **B** CORK ON CROWQUILL SPECIAL

C TRADITIONAL AVON FLOAT

4 LB BS TO ROD

ALL FLOATS FIXED TOP AND BOTTOM WITH SILICON TUBING

FLOW

FLOW

BULK SHOT 12 IN FROM HOOK

HOOK SIZES 14 TO 10 TIED DIRECT

FOR FAST SHALLOW SWIMS

BOTTOM SILICON TUBING OVERLAPS BOTTOM OF FLOAT BY 1/4 IN

BULK SHOT OF AA IN LINE 2–3 FT FROM HOOK

BULK SHOT 2–3 FT ABOVE HOOK

NO. 3 OR NO. 1 SHOT

BB OR AA SHOT

HOOKS 14 TO 10 TIED DIRECT TO REEL LINE

HOOKS 14 TO 10 TIED DIRECT TO REEL LINE

change floats or hooks. My waistcoat is loaded up with a box of hooks and shots, float bands, a wallet of floats, forceps, plummets and a few spools of mono lighter than the reel line for those extra-shy or spooky barbel.

FIGURE 24 *Long-trotting rigs*

I generally opt for a trotting line of around 4 lb test, and I have already mentioned (see p. 48) my preference for trotting using a centre-pin reel. This I use in conjunction with a 13 ft, carbon waggler rod, but for tackling swims with particularly heavy weed, bullrushes or an extra strong flow, I increase the power to a 12 ft, 1¼ lb test curve, carbon Avon, which harmonizes nicely with a 5 lb or 6 lb test line.

Really shallow, fast runs are most effectively fished with a short, fat float (long floats could easily spook the barbel) such as the chubber, with all the shot bulked 12 in above the hook (see fig. 24A). These floats have a wide tip and can be easily seen at distances up to 30 yd. Keep running the float through unchecked, inching it up the line on each cast until the bait is dragging bottom so hard that the float pulls under. Then pull it down a shade and commence fishing. This is a far easier method of finding the depth than plumbing the entire length of the swim.

In deep, steady runs where extra shots down the line are imperative for presenting the bait smoothly and trundling it along in a natural manner, I use cork on crowquill floats. These specials take up to 6AA and are best rigged with most of the bulk-shot loading set in a line 2–3 ft above the hook with a No. 1 or a No. 3 between it and the hook (see fig. 24B) – simple but most effective.

When the water is deep and swirling, the float to use is the traditional Avon. Its bulbous, oval body and thick tip permit maximum shotting capacity for a stable trot through and ensure that the bait searches slowly, close to or actually along the river-bed (fig. oo). To achieve the correct depth, follow the procedure for chubbers. In really long swims, however, of 20 or 30 yd, it is not uncommon to find a raised lump on the bottom that would present the bait too high throughout most of the trot if it is set to the shallowest depth. The remedy is to hold back hard on the float just before the hump or similar obstruction (such as a weed clump) to ease the end tackle over it and then continue the rest of the run through.

Close-range trotting

As all long trotting enthusiasts are only too aware, a tinge of colour in the river following overnight rain will cause barbel to feed in earnest.

When bank fishing, and for presenting the bait along the bottom of swims where there is little venom in the current pace, I like the sensitivity of big sticks and balsa trotters. I even step down to a 3 lb reel line if there are no snags or marginal rushes and reeds.

The shotting load can be spread evenly in three or four groups (depending on swim depth), with a small shot, a No. 4 or 6, between the lowest group and the hook (fig. 25). Try slightly overshotting the float so that you can ease back gently (as though stick-float fishing for roach) all the way down the swim with a fairly controlled line from rod to float tip. Do not be afraid to set the float well over-depth so the bait literally bumps bottom all the way down the swim. Bites are invariably a bold sinking of the tip which looks exactly like the bottom.

If the water runs crystal clear and bites on a heavier set up do not happen although you are certain fish are in the swim, be prepared to step down to small hooks, sizes 16 and 18 on a 2 lb bottom, as long as you have room to play

FIGURE 25 *Close-range trotting with big-stick/balsa trotter rigs*

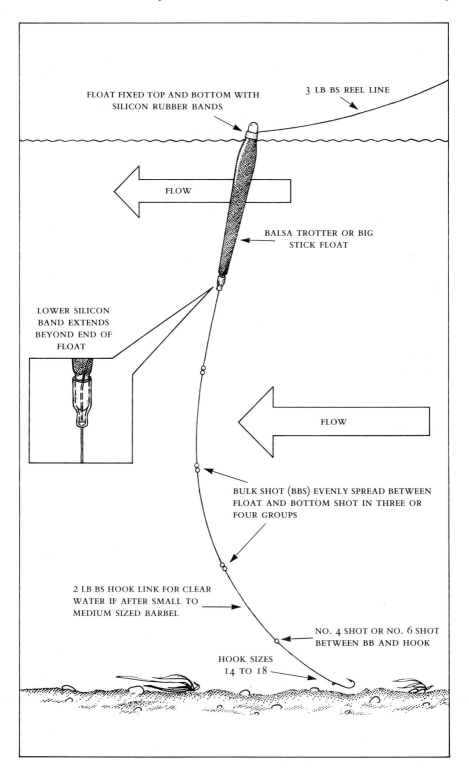

FLOAT FIXED TOP AND BOTTOM WITH
SILICON RUBBER BANDS

3 LB BS REEL LINE

FLOW

BALSA TROTTER OR BIG
STICK FLOAT

LOWER SILICON
BAND EXTENDS
BEYOND END OF
FLOAT

FLOW

BULK SHOT (BBS) EVENLY SPREAD BETWEEN
FLOAT AND BOTTOM SHOT IN THREE OR
FOUR GROUPS

2 LB BS HOOK LINK FOR CLEAR
WATER IF AFTER SMALL TO
MEDIUM SIZED BARBEL

NO. 4 SHOT OR NO. 6 SHOT
BETWEEN BB AND HOOK

HOOK SIZES
14 TO 18

FIGURE 26 *Waggler
fishing – peacock
waggler rigs.*

the barbel without the problems caused by nearby snags. I
am talking here about small to medium-sized barbel, up to
4–5 lb. If there is any chance whatsoever of a specimen
barbel inhabiting the swim, my advice is to stick with the
tackle capable of landing it should you hook one. Skilful
match fishermen seem to get away with murder using
gossamer-fine tackle, and eventually manage to subdue
specimen fish of most species. However, hooking a fair-
sized barbel on inadequate tackle is not to be encouraged.
For every one landed, there are inevitably several lost
trailing end-rigs. And even if eventually beaten, the fish is
liable to be unacceptably knackered. In high water
temperatures it could end up on its last legs.

Waggler fishing

Owing to the distance involved in reaching certain swims
with float tackle, even after wading out a few yards,
natural presentation of the bait can be hampered by a float
fixed top and bottom. Any kind of control, or the slightest
wind, will drag the float and consequently the bait off the
feed line, across the swim instead of down it. Then, the
obvious remedy is to fish the waggler. Indeed, on certain
barbel rivers it is *the* method.

For ease of casting, and to hit the same line consistently,
do not be afraid to rig up a really big, thick peacock
waggler that takes plenty of shot. Between 5AA and 6AA.
For long, medium-paced swims where there is time for the
bait to find its level slowly, bulk most of the shot around
the float, leaving room down below for a couple of No. 1s
and a No. 4 20 in above the hook (see fig. 26). In order
every so often to mend the bow that forms between rod-
tip and float as it is carried downstream unchecked, grease
the line above the float with mucilin. The bow is
impossible to mend if the line is sunk.

If the bottom is clean, smooth sand or gravel, the float
tip may be shotted reasonably well down. Where the river
bed is uneven, however, leave a good 1½ in of the tip
above the surface, encouraging the buoyancy in the
peacock waggler to drag the bait over the river-bed
without the tip being submerged. When a barbel inhales
the bait, you will be in absolutely no doubt of a bite. In

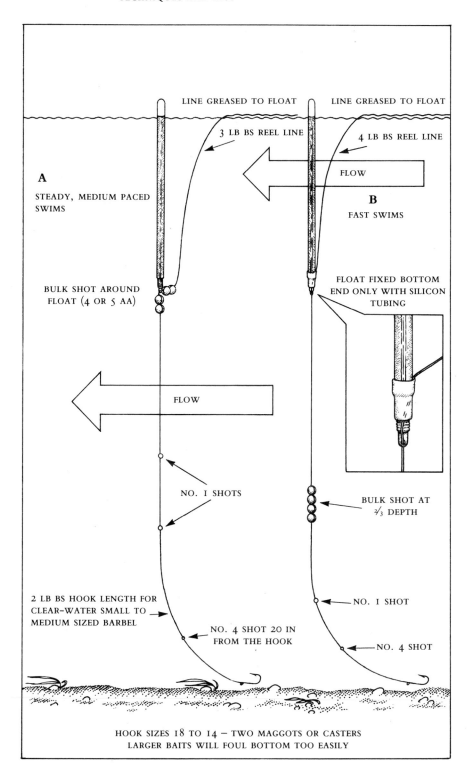

LINE GREASED TO FLOAT   LINE GREASED TO FLOAT

3 LB BS REEL LINE

4 LB BS REEL LINE

FLOW

A

STEADY, MEDIUM PACED
SWIMS

B

FAST SWIMS

BULK SHOT AROUND
FLOAT (4 OR 5 AA)

FLOAT FIXED BOTTOM
END ONLY WITH SILICON
TUBING

FLOW

NO. 1 SHOTS

BULK SHOT AT
⅔ DEPTH

2 LB BS HOOK LENGTH FOR
CLEAR-WATER SMALL TO
MEDIUM SIZED BARBEL

NO. 1 SHOT

NO. 4 SHOT 20 IN
FROM THE HOOK

NO. 4 SHOT

HOOK SIZES 18 TO 14 – TWO MAGGOTS OR CASTERS
LARGER BAITS WILL FOUL BOTTOM TOO EASILY

*Dave Wilson hooks
into a nice barbel
while waggler fishing
a bunch of maggots
down a wide, shallow
section of the River
Lea Relief Channel.*

really clear water, the hook link can be reduced to make spooky fish bite, but no lighter than 2 lb test. Remember to keep feeding exactly the same line with the catapult on every cast to ensure that barbel move over the bait at some point along the swim. A loose feed mixture of hemp and casters works well in clear water with double caster, caster and maggot or double maggot on the hook.

To waggler-fish fast swims, shallow or deep, I prefer to bulk most of the shots at around two-thirds depth, with a No. 1 and a No. 4 between them and the hook. The float is not locked to the line in the normal way, but held tightly by silicone tubing. I also feel happier switching over from a 3 lb to a 4 lb reel line in stronger currents – and ensure the line for at least 5 or 6 yd immediately above the float has a liberal coating of mucilin.

Lastly, it is perhaps worth pointing out that the larger the bait used, the more chance there is of it fouling bottom. You can get away with lobworm tails or a lump of bread flake where the bottom is smooth sand or fine gravel by undershotting the float even less. However, with any kind of inconsistency along the river-bed in the way of rocks, decaying stubble or weed, light, small baits such as maggots and casters are the order of the day. The only exception being a $\frac{1}{4}$ in cube of breadcrust, which has enormous inherent buoyancy. This is a fine barbel bait to try when the river is tinged with winter green and the weather is mild. Mix up some mashed bread (see page 90) and lob a tightly squeezed golfball into the head of the run every few casts to start the barbel moving. On the retrieve, the crust will naturally have departed and this after several casts will in itself create loose feed. So be miserly with the mash.

Good barbel fishing, and hang on!

INDEX

FATHER & SON

The world's biggest selling angling weekly publication has now launched the best selling fishing monthly. So join the family and get the best of both worlds...the latest news and views every Wednesday in *Angling Times*...the top advice and instruction in *Improve Your Coarse Fishing* every month.

Everything you need to know about coarse fishing is covered by these two publications...they make the perfect combination.

The No I for.......
- Form guides
- Latest tackle reviews
- Hot news stories
- Fishery spotlights
- Match reports
- Features

The No I for.......
- Hints and tips
- Facts on bait
- Species spotlights
- Fish-catching rigs
- In-depth tackle trials
- Which guides